Webber®

Hear It! Say It! Learn It!™

Speech Sound Awareness and Phonics Program with Interactive CD-ROM

Resource Book 1
Letter Sounds: B, F, M, T, G, P, D, and K/C

Interactive CD-ROM

Super Duper® Publications

T5-AFP-751

Based Upon the *Beginning Reading Through Speech* Approach Developed by Adele Gerber, M.A., CCC-SLP

by Adele Gerber, M.A., CCC-SLP
Evelyn R. Klein, Ph.D., CCC-SLP
Jenny Roberts, Ph.D., CCC-SLP

Contributing Authors
Susie S. Loraine, M.A., CCC-SLP and Mark Strait, M.Ed., CCC-SLP

Printed in the United States

Book Design by Jessica Horton

Cover by Bill Golliher

Artwork by Tim Davis

ISBN 1-58650-915-2

Super Duper® Publications
www.superduperinc.com
Post Office Box 24997 • Greenville, SC 29616 USA
1-800-277-8737 • Fax 1-800-978-7379

About the Authors

Adele Gerber, M.A., CCC-SLP, Professor Emeritus
Temple University, Philadelphia, Pennsylvania

Adele Gerber is Professor Emeritus at Temple University in Philadelphia, Pennsylvania, where she served on the faculty in the Department of Communication Sciences and Disorders for 20 years. Her early training and experience was in Education, followed by a career in Speech-Language Pathology. She is a Fellow of the American Speech-Language-Hearing Association (ASHA).

Over the course of her tenure at Temple, her publications, national and local conference presentations, and her academic coursework evolved in an interdisciplinary direction, culminating in the publication of the text *Language-Related Learning Disabilities: Their Nature and Treatment*, which was translated into Portuguese for publication in Brazil. She has continued her professional activity after retirement from Temple University, serving as consultant and collaborator, largely but not exclusively, under the auspices of RSVP (Retired and Senior Volunteer Program). She received a Points of Light Award for her volunteer services and was honored by Temple with a Distinguished Alumni Award in the year 2000. In 2005, she received the Janet L. Hoopes Award from the Philadelphia Branch of the International Dyslexia Association (IDA), an award given for her significant contribution to the advancement of the education of those with learning disabilities.

In 1998, in response to the call of the United States Government's *America Reads*, she revised her longstanding program, *Beginning Reading Through Speech*, in collaboration with Evelyn Klein, Ph.D., Assistant Professor at LaSalle University, and later, in further collaboration with Jenny Roberts, Ph.D., Assistant Professor at Hofstra University.

In 2001, she trained a group of teachers in the Norristown Area School District in the use of this program. After implementing *Beginning Reading Through Speech* in first and second grades for children testing below basic level on the *Houghton-Mifflin Test of Emergent Literacy,* these children achieved Basic or Proficient levels on all subtests after 5 months of after-hours training.

Evelyn R. Klein, Ph.D., CCC-SLP, BRS-CL
Associate Professor, La Salle University, Philadelphia, Pennsylvania

Dr. Evelyn R. Klein is Associate Professor of Speech-Language-Hearing Science at La Salle University in Philadelphia, Pennsylvania. She is a licensed and certified speech-language pathologist and licensed psychologist with post-doctoral training in neuropsychology. She holds Board Specialty Recognition in Child Language from the American Speech-Language-Hearing Association and has Supervisory Certification in Special Education from the Pennsylvania Department of Education.

Dr. Klein is a teacher, clinician, and researcher. She teaches, supervises, and advises undergraduate and graduate students pursuing degrees in speech-language pathology. Her areas of specialization include language-learning disabilities, acquired language disorders, research design, and counseling for communicative disorders. For more than 25 years, she has evaluated and treated children, teens, and adults with communication disorders and learning differences, as well as behavior and anxiety disorders.

About the Authors

Evelyn R. Klein, Ph.D., CCC-SLP, BRS-CL (Cont.)

She maintains a private practice in speech-language pathology and psychology. Dr. Klein is also involved in research investigating visual-verbal associations and working memory in children with and without reading disorders. She is currently investigating new models for assessing children with selective mutism. Other recent work has involved the use of cognitive behavioral therapy for people who stutter.

Dr. Klein has been the principal investigator for several research grants funded through the United States Department of Education. She is co-creator of the MAGIC Program, (Maximizing Academic Growth by Improving Communication), which provides assessment and treatment to elementary school students who need support in reading, writing, listening, and speaking. She also developed the Early Childhood Inclusion Support Program, for young children throughout the mid-Atlantic region, to enhance cognition and language skills.

Dr. Klein prides herself in mentoring undergraduate and graduate students to develop their own research. She continues to publish in peer-reviewed journals and presents her work at local, national, and international conferences. She also published the popular Focus On Function series, providing treatment for teens and adults with acquired language disorders.

Jenny Roberts, Ph.D., CCC-SLP
Associate Professor, Hofstra University, Hempstead, New York

Dr. Jenny Roberts is Associate Professor of Speech-Language-Hearing Science at Hofstra University in Hempstead, New York. Her current research focus is on the early identification and treatment of children at risk for specific language impairments, including later written language impairments. Dr. Roberts is also a member of a team of researchers investigating the origins of dyslexia in children at genetic risk for the disorder. This longitudinal study, in progress for over 14 years, has resulted in numerous presentations and scholarly publications.

In Philadelphia, Dr. Roberts and Ms. Gerber adapted the *Beginning Reading Through Speech* program as a stand-alone "Sound Story Book," which was provided as an intervention to children at risk of reading failure and their caretakers. The Sound Story Book promotes phonological awareness and letter identification in preschool aged children. The Sound Story Book is now in use in a variety of clinics and preschools in the Eastern United States.

Dr. Roberts teaches courses in reading development and disorders, as well as courses in phonetics, language acquisition, and child language disorders. She has conducted numerous literacy and teacher-training workshops for the education and speech-language pathology communities. She is a developmental psychologist and certified speech-language pathologist, specializing in the assessment and intervention of spoken and written language disorders. She has also published extensively in the area of international adoption.

#BKCD-407 Webber® Hear It! Say It! Learn It!™ • ©2008 Super Duper® Publications • www.superduperinc.com • 1-800-277-8737

About the Contributing Authors

Susie S. Loraine, M.A., CCC-SLP

Susie S. Loraine, M.A., CCC-SLP received a Master of Arts degree in Speech-Language Pathology at the University of Kansas in 2001. Her experience as a speech-language pathologist includes working in a multidisciplinary diagnostic clinic for children with a wide variety of developmental disabilities, providing home intervention for infants and toddlers, including parent training and education, and providing speech/language/ auditory services in an educational setting. She has specialized in working with children who are deaf or hard-of-hearing and children with multiple disabilities. She is currently an Editor at Super Duper® Publications where her work includes the development of products and tests, including the *Montgomery Assessment of Vocabulary Acquisition*™ and the *Social Emotional Evaluation*™.

Mark Strait, M.Ed., CCC-SLP

Mark Strait, M.Ed., CCC-SLP is the head of Multimedia Development at Super Duper® Publications. Mark received a Master of Education degree in Communication Sciences and Disorders from the University of Georgia in 1993. He practiced speech-language pathology in inpatient, outpatient, and home healthcare settings before returning to the University of Georgia in 2000 to earn a Master of Education in Instructional Technology. Mark began work at Super Duper® Publications in 2001 and has developed several multimedia programs including *Auditory Memory for Quick Stories, Webber® Interactive "WH" Questions CD-ROM Levels 1 and 2*, and *"Sort and Say"*™ *Early Classifying Interactive Games CD-ROM*.

Table of Contents

Book 1

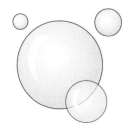

#BKCD-407 Webber® Hear It! Say It! Learn It!™ • ©2008 Super Duper® Publications • www.superduperinc.com • 1-800-277-8737

Table of Contents

Introduction

Webber® *Hear It! Say It! Learn It!*™ (based upon the *Beginning Reading Through Speech* approach by Adele Gerber) is an interactive, evidence-based, speech and language program that teaches 16 speech sounds and phonemic awareness—plus phonics. The easy-to-follow scripted lessons and engaging software help students listen for, say, and recognize high-frequency English speech sounds and their corresponding letters. After intensive speech sound training and auditory bombardment, the students learn the letter(s) that represent each sound, how to recognize the letters in words, and how to write them.

Hear It! Say It! Learn It!™ includes:

- Two Program Resource Books (384 pages total)

- Interactive CD-ROM with an additional six (6) activities for each of the 16 chapters, data tracking for an unlimited number of students, and printable versions of Resource Books 1 and 2.

Hear It! Say It! Learn It!™ focuses on the 16 most frequently occurring simple consonants in the initial positions of English words (B, F, M, T, G, P, D, K/C, H, V, N, W, L, S, R, and J). Q, X, and Z do not appear because of the infrequency of their occurrence in CVC (consonant-vowel-consonant) written words. Digraphs and blends are omitted because they reflect a higher level of complexity beyond the scope of this program.

Chapters in the *Resource Books* begin by teaching students to listen for and then say the target speech sound. The program pairs each speech sound to an icon rather than a letter (the /b/ sound is the Bubble Sound; the /d/ sound is the Drum Sound). These "Sound Pictures" are a type of visual "anchor," an important multi-sensory component of the program. This visual component is important because coarticulation in speech can make it difficult for students to become auditorily aware of individual phonemes.

Next, the students make a flashcard that has the icon on one side and the letter on the other. Then, the students listen to an auditory bombardment story that is loaded with that sound. *Hear It! Say It! Learn It!*™ progresses from sound awareness to decoding of CVC (consonant-vowel-consonant) words in print. The program introduces letters in the second half of each chapter—after the students have a high level of awareness of the speech sounds. The last part of each chapter works to secure awareness and knowledge of speech sounds, as well as sound-letter correspondence and the application of these skills for reading simple CVC words and writing the letters.

The interactive software tracks data on an unlimited number of students and is excellent reinforcement for six of the lessons in each chapter. The students may also listen to the sound-loaded stories on the CD-ROM while viewing three illustrated scenes. Extension Activities follow the completion of each chapter and foster the integration of speech sound and letter awareness in "top-down," meaning-generating processes.

Hear It! Say It! Learn It!™ also includes assessments for progress monitoring. Use the quick tests at the beginning of the program, at the midpoint, and at the end. The tests are great for identifying students that may require special education services or need additional help in the classroom.

#BKCD-407 Webber® Hear It! Say It! Learn It!™ • ©2008 Super Duper® Publications • www.superduperinc.com • 1-800-277-8737

Target Sounds and Icons

Bubble Sound /b/	Frisky Cat Sound /f/	Humming Sound /m/	Time Sound /t/
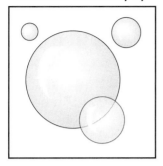			
Baby Sound /g/	Popcorn Sound /p/	Drum Sound /d/	Rooster Sound /k/

Happy Sound /h/	Vacuum Sound /v/	No Sound /n/	Puppy Sound /w/

Singing Sound /l/	Snake Sound /s/	Roaring Sound /r/	Jumping Sound /ʤ/ (J)

Chapter Sequence

Chapter Introduction

Introduction of the Target Sound — The teacher or SLP introduces the target sound using the script at the beginning of each chapter. The script encourages students to pay close attention to the visual, auditory, and kinesthetic features (multisensory perception) of the target speech sound, and to practice producing the sound. Each chapter introduction includes examples of questions to help facilitate increased multisensory awareness of the sound. (Descriptions of Consonant Sound Productions for the SLP/Teacher are in *Resource Book 2*, Appendix A.)

Note: The letter name is not discussed at this stage in the program, only the sound itself, a picture icon, and name that accompanies the icon.

Picture Icon Cutout

Introduction of Picture Icons — Following the introduction to the target sound, the teacher or SLP presents a picture icon to represent the sound. For example, a picture of bubbles is used to represent the plosive /b/ and a picture of a snake is presented to represent the continuant sibilant /s/. The students make a large, Picture Symbol Flashcard to help to associate the sound with its picture.

Auditory Bombardment Story

Sound Bombardment Through Meaningful Stories — Following the introduction of a new consonant sound and its icon, the teacher or SLP reads the sound story aloud or plays it from the CD-ROM. The stories are loaded with the target sound and include multiple occasions of the sound in isolation. Auditory bombardment of the target sound, woven into the story plot, heightens awareness of the consonant features, such as a restriction of airflow followed by a burst of air for the plosive sound of /p/. Embedding the target sound in a story about popcorn prepares the student to associate the sound (/p/) with its picture icon (popcorn) and its label (The Popping Sound).

The sounds are carefully sequenced throughout the program so that they can be made maximally contrastive to one another, thus reducing potential confusion for the student. For example, an early sound that is introduced is /m/, the "Humming Sound," which is a voiced, nasal sound produced with the lips closed. It is learned after an unvoiced, fricative sound /f/, the "Frisky Cat Sound," produced with the teeth and bottom lip.

 Auditory Bombardment Story — Student(s) listens to the story accompanied by illustrations. The teacher or SLP chooses to play the story with or without text.

Worksheet 1

Sound Discrimination in Isolation — Student(s) practices recognition and discrimination of the isolated target sound.

 Giraffe Task - Isolation — Student(s) plays the interactive game to practice recognition and discrimination of the isolated target sound.

Worksheet 2

Sound Discrimination in Syllables — After the student(s) demonstrates the ability to recognize the target sound in isolation, and associate it with the picture icon, Worksheet 2 introduces consonant-vowel (CV) syllables, minimally increasing the complexity of the stimuli without the distraction of word meaning.

 Monkey Task - Syllables — Student(s) plays the interactive game to practice recognition and discrimination of the target sound in syllables.

Worksheet 3

Sound Discrimination in Real Words — Complexity is increased by using real, meaningful, single-syllable words. For example, the student identifies which of two pictured words begins with the "Bubble Sound /b/"—sock or bell.

#BKCD-407 Webber® Hear It! Say It! Learn It!™ • ©2008 Super Duper® Publications • www.superduperinc.com • 1-800-277-8737

Bear Task - Real Words — Student(s) plays the interactive game to practice recognition and discrimination of the target sound in pictures of real words.

Introduction to the Letter

Letter Introduction — Once the student(s) has established strong phonemic awareness of the target sound, the teacher or SLP introduces both the uppercase and lowercase forms of the target letter and instructions for writing them. At this point, the student(s) makes the Letter Flashcard. This aspect of introducing the letter, only after sound awareness is established, is one of several characteristics that distinguish this approach from other methods of teaching beginning reading.

Worksheet 4

Forming the Letter — Student(s) practices writing the uppercase and lowercase forms of the letter.

Note: Students under 5 years old may not be developmentally ready for the handwriting activities.

Worksheet 5

Identifying the Sound and Isolated Letter — After becoming visually aware of the target letter, the student(s) will listen for the target sound and choose from a pair of pictures accompanied by the initial letter of each word. The target letter is randomly shown in uppercase and lowercase forms throughout the activity to ensure recognition of both forms.

 Elephant Task - Pictures with Isolated Letter — Student(s) plays the interactive game to practice recognition and discrimination of the target sound in pictures of real words accompanied by the initial letter of each word.

Worksheet 6

Printing Letters — Student(s) prints the letter in the picture upon hearing the target sound in isolation.

Worksheet 7

Letter-Sound Correspondence in Printed Words — Student(s) looks at two CVC words next to picture representations and identifies which word contains the target sound. The target letter only appears in the initial position of each word and is bold each time it appears to minimally increase difficulty and facilitate success.

 Penguin Task - Pictures with Word — Student(s) plays the interactive game to practice recognition and discrimination of the target sound in pictures with words.

Worksheet 8

Beginning Reading — Student(s) listens and looks at printed CVC words without the support of pictures or bold letters. Student(s) will identify which word begins with the target sound and its corresponding letter.

 Seal Task - Words — Student(s) plays the interactive game to practice recognition and discrimination of the target sound and corresponding letter in real words.

Extension Activity

Experience-Content Stories — At the conclusion of each chapter, there is an optional extension activity which incorporates the target sound and letter. The activities are meaningful and perfect for carry-over and generalization. The teacher or SLP should encourage the student(s) to retell the activity and write the statements on an easel or chalkboard. This gives the student(s) a chance to practice identifying the sound and letter in a brief passage of conected meaningful text, which leads to early success in decoding and comprehending print.

Interactive CD-ROM

 Playground Activities — At the end of each unit (four chapters), student(s) plays two interactive games to review all of the icons, sounds, and letters from that unit. These games are played prior to the unit assessment.

Full Program Sequence

For each sound, the process is the same. All of the worksheets should be completed sequentially until the student has achieved at least 80% (approximately 8 out of 10 items) correct on each worksheet. Note that within each unit, scoresheets 1, 2, and 5 provide additional sets of practice items if a student needs extra practice.

Initial Assessment of Letter/Sound knowledge

- **List of Assessments** - *Book 2, p. 165*
- **Assessment Section** - *Book 2, pp. 166–173*

Unit 1

- **Bubble Sound /b/** - *Book 1, pp. 3–22*
- **Frisky Cat Sound /f/** - *Book 1, pp. 23–42*
- **Humming Sound /m/** - *Book 1, pp. 43–62*
- **Time sound /t/** - *Book 1, pp. 63–82*
- **Unit 1 Review: Playground Activities** - Interactive CD-ROM
- **Unit 1 Assessment: Assessment Section** - *Book 2, pp. 176–177*

Unit 2

- **Baby Sound /g/** - *Book 1, pp. 85–104*
- **Popcorn Sound /p/** - *Book 1, pp. 105–124*
- **Drum Sound /d/** - *Book 1, pp. 125–144*
- **Rooster Sound /k/** - *Book 1, pp. 145–168*
- **Unit 2 Review: Playground Activities** - Interactive CD-ROM
- **Unit 2 Assessment: Assessment Section** - *Book 2, pp. 178–179*

Midway Review Assessment

- **Assessment Section** - *Book 2, pp. 180–181*

Unit 3

- **Happy Sound /h/** - *Book 2, pp. 3–22*
- **Vacuum Sound /v/** - *Book 2, pp. 23–42*
- **No Sound /n/** - *Book 2, pp. 43–62*
- **Puppy Sound /w/** - *Book 2, pp. 63–82*
- **Unit 3 Review: Playground Activities** - Interactive CD-ROM
- **Unit 3 Assessment: Assessment Section** - *Book 2, pp. 182–183*

Unit 4

- **Singing Sound /l/** - *Book 2, pp. 85–104*
- **Snake Sound /s/** - *Book 2, pp. 105–124*
- **Roaring Sound /r/** - *Book 2, pp. 125–144*
- **Jumping Sound /ʤ/ (J)** - *Book 2, pp. 145–164*
- **Unit 4 Review: Playground Activities** - Interactive CD-ROM
- **Unit 4 Assessment: Assessment Section** - *Book 2, pp. 184–185*

Final Review Assessment

- **Assessment Section** - *Book 2, pp. 186–188*

Letter Identification (ID)

- **Assessment Section** - *Book 2, pp. 168–170*

Sound Identification (ID)

- **Assessment Section** - *Book 2, pp. 171–173*

*Note: for a complete assessment chart and detailed assessment procedures, see p. 166.

Theory and Research

In general, the spoken form of a native language is acquired without instruction, however, the acquisition of reading and writing skills almost always requires direct instruction. This is because reading is a complex process that presents a demanding challenge, not only for those learning to read, but for those fostering the process (Moats, 1999). To successfully teach reading, it is imperative for instructors to have a comprehensive understanding of language.

The Reading-Language Connection

Reading is the ability to process language in a written form. Reading consists of two components: decoding and comprehension. *Decoding* is the ability to recognize and read words by converting letters into speech sounds to determine pronunciation. *Comprehension* is the ability to gain meaning from words that are read. Before students can begin to easily decode words, they must understand the relationship between speech sounds and written symbols of sounds (i.e., letters and letter combinations). A child's oral language skills influence his/her ability to both decode and comprehend written language. One way to understand how language is organized is to look at five levels of linguistic knowledge.

Levels of Linguistic Knowledge

I. Phonological System

A *phonological system* is an inventory of all the sounds included in a particular language, as well as the permissible combinations of these sounds into meaningful units. For example, tongue-clicks are not included in the English language phonological system and /ŋ/ does not occur at the beginning of English words.

II. Word Forms [Morphological Knowledge]

Word forms consist of the way sounds are combined into meaningful units. The smallest meaningful units of sounds are called *morphemes*. There are two types of morphemes—free and bound. *Free morphemes* include units that stand alone (e.g., walk); *bound morphemes* include units affixed to free morphemes that change their meaning (e.g., walk + ed = walked).

III. Word Knowledge

Word knowledge requires associative networks that store the meanings of words and the relationships among them. For example, the word "cat" may conjure numerous combinations of concepts or schema.

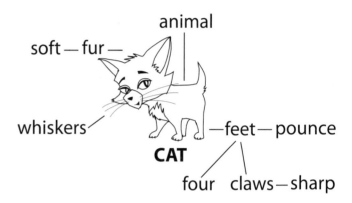

Semantic knowledge refers to the way meaning is derived from words in sentences in combination with the stored knowledge of relationships among words and concepts. For example, there are many cognitive concepts expressed semantically. These may include:

- Similarities (synonyms) = big – large

- Opposites (antonyms) = hot – cold

- Association = window – glass

- Categories = animals – cow, pig, horse

- Figurative vs. Literal = hard-hearted vs. hard rock

IV. Syntactic Knowledge

Syntax incorporates the rules that determine how words are ordered into phrasal, clausal, and sentence groups in any particular language. For example, in English, an article precedes rather than follows a noun (e.g., "the cat" versus "cat the"). A noun phrase normally precedes a verb phrase (e.g., The cat ran away).

V. World Knowledge

World knowledge is acquired through information stored in long-term memory that has been experienced through real-life interaction with the environment and derived vicariously from accounts of the experiences of others, either in written or spoken discourse.

Understanding Reading

The reading components previously described show the correlation between written language and an individual's spoken language abilities. Because reading is primarily a language activity, a deficit in any of the above language-based skills could impact a person's ability to read.

The ability to decode words, the critical skill of beginning reading, has been found to be much more dependent upon an individual's *phonological abilities*—the ability to detect, manipulate, store, and use the sounds of the language to ultimately create sound-letter correspondences and "crack the alphabetic code" (Liberman, 1997). Once word identification becomes quicker and less time is spent decoding words, children can devote their mental energy applying meaning to the words they read.

However, meaning will not occur if the individual does not have stored knowledge of the words and concepts conveyed by this code. In the semantic analysis of "cat" (p. xiii), the word "pounce," once decoded, will make little sense to a reader if he/she does not understand that this word refers to the cat's movements. Semantics, syntax, world knowledge, and morphological knowledge all contribute greatly to an individual's ability to gather meaning from the printed word.

The processing of speech sounds in both oral and written modalities involves heightened awareness of a single speech sound in isolation. In speech, the isolated sound is called a *phone*, and the smallest meaningful segment of a word is a *phoneme*. For example, the sound /b/ when added to "oy," makes *boy* while a /t/ makes it *toy*. By changing a single phoneme, we can change the meaning of words. In written language (both reading and writing), this isolated segment is represented most often by a letter (although exceptions such as "ph" can occur). The beginning reader's task is to perceive individual speech sounds and then map these sounds into letters.

Phonemic Awareness and the Segmentation Challenge: Coarticulation

A word such as "pat" is perceived auditorily as a single burst of sound, but is visually perceived as three separate letters. This disparity is due to the speech phenomenon of *coarticulation* (i.e., several phonemes merge together without any overt segmentation, and are perceived as a single sound; Liberman, 1997; Shaywitz, 2003). The task of segmenting words confronts early language users with a primary obstacle—distinguishing the distinct speech sounds within a coarticulated word. Readers need to reverse this skill to decode words. *Decoding* requires pairing letters that are visually separated to sounds that overlap seamlessly when spoken. Thus, learning to read is fundamentally different from learning to talk.

Metalinguistic awareness, or the ability to consciously reflect upon language, does not ensure spontaneous awareness of speech sounds—phonemes—very small linguistic units. Most words are composed of multiple phonemes. In conversational speech, listeners attend to the message of the speaker, rather than the linguistic units that carry the message. Pre-readers must become aware that words are composed of

#BKCD-407 Webber® Hear It! Say It! Learn It!!™ • ©2008 Super Duper® Publications • www.superduperinc.com • 1-800-277-8737 individual speech sounds; this critical awareness leads to the ability to decode the written form of a language.

Research has demonstrated that the tasks of phonemic awareness and decoding are not effortless for all early readers. For example, the basic neural mechanism that is deficient in individuals with dyslexia appears to be at the phonemic level (Shaywitz, et al., 2002; Paulesu, et al., 2001). Children with dyslexia have a deficit in the phonological component of language (i.e., difficulty in the ability to accurately identify and represent speech sounds). This results in poor decoding and spelling skills.

Instructional Processes

Researchers have identified that phonological awareness, spoken language ability, and letter identification abilities in the preschool years are the best predictors of later reading ability (Catts, Fey, Tomblin, & Zhang, 2002; Scarborough, 1998; Sweet, 2000; Torgensen, Wagner, & Rashotte, 1994). Predictors of word-reading ability in the first grade are related to phonological sensitivity to speech sounds, word onsets, rimes, and syllables. The National Reading Panel (2000) documented a positive relationship among letter knowledge, phonemic awareness (i.e., speech-sound sensitivity), and early reading achievement. The National Reading Panel's definition of *phonemic awareness training* involves teaching pre-readers to discriminate and manipulate phonemes in syllables and words.

Phonemic awareness training tasks are distinct and vary in effectiveness depending on stage of development. *Phonemic awareness* is the ability to discriminate and manipulate individual sounds in words—this includes adding, deleting, or segmenting these sounds. For example, in one study of kindergarten children by Abbot, Walton, and Greenwood (2002), systematic, analytic

training resulted in gains in identifying the first consonant sound in a word (i.e., perception of single consonant onset) and in letter-naming. However, on phonemic segmentation tasks in which children were required to divide a whole word into its separate phonemic parts, performance declined. In addition, school principals found that the teachers themselves were opposed to the use of phonemic segmentation tasks, claiming that such tasks exceeded their students' developmental capabilities, especially at the kindergarten level.

Many traditional reading programs assume young readers can identify sounds embedded in words, as well as segment the sounds and blend them back into words. Introduction of the letter also often occurs very early in a traditional instructional approach. For example, program approaches that incorporate letters embedded in words, such as *A is for apple, B is for ball*, etc. assume that the child can detect the sound as an isolated part of a word and understand that letters represent speech sounds. Decoding depends on understanding the critical relationship between sounds and letters. Yet, traditional instruction often begins with an assumed level of phonological awareness too difficult for some children to achieve (e.g., phoneme segmentation in words), and/or with letter identification prior to children understanding the function of the letter.

In comparison with these approaches, **Webber®** **Hear It! Say It! Learn It!**™ uses a speech-based approach to initiate the process of phonemic awareness before the establishment of sound-letter correspondence. In order to pair a speech sound with a corresponding letter in early reading, the student must be able to perceive sound segments or phonemes in words. This approach promotes intense speech sound awareness before introducing corresponding letters. To facilitate this deep awareness of speech sounds,

sounds are first presented in isolation—that is, lifted out of surrounding context so that attention may be focused on the characteristics of the sound production. This is in contrast to perception of the whole word to which meaning is attached.

Webber® Hear It! Say It! Learn It!™ initiates training with the *phone*—the isolated speech sound—as opposed to the *phoneme*—which is the sound embedded within the word. The use of the phone rather than the phoneme as the initial unit of instruction is a crucial difference from other approaches to reading instruction. This approach leads the child to begin reading by first identifying speech sounds that will later be mapped to letters. Phonemic segmentation tasks, which require the child to "pull apart" sounds before readily understanding them, are not used until sound knowledge is secure.

Once again, reading consists of two important components: decoding and comprehension. A large emphasis of the **Hear It! Say It! Learn It!**™ program ensures that decoded words are inserted in meaningful contexts by engaging children in activities that focus on both linguistic form and content. This allows the reader to construct meaning from print, which is the ultimate goal for reading.

The **Hear It! Say It! Learn It!**™ program includes extension activities at the completion of each phoneme/letter chapter. The teacher or SLP facilitates meaningful, sound-loaded activities, then leads the student(s) in discussion about the activity and records statements. Finally the teacher or SLP and student(s) read aloud the "story" about the activity. These experiences provide an opportunity to increase awareness of the target sound and letter, as well as build vocabulary.

Program Results

The *Beginning Reading Through Speech* approach was used with a group of first and second grade teachers in an urban school from 2000–2001. The program was implemented with 38 students who scored Below Basic (including 7 students who were developmentally delayed) on the pretest of the Houghton-Mifflin Test of Emergent Literacy in September of 2000. In groups of 3–5 students, over a 6 month period, all students improved in all 12 areas tested, moving from Below Basic into the Basic and Proficient levels of early reading skills. These 12 areas included:

1. rhyme
2. beginning sounds
3. blending onsets and rhymes
4. concepts of print
5. letter naming
6. segmenting onsets and rhymes
7. phoneme blending
8. phoneme segmenting
9. word recognition
10. fluency
11. word writing
12. sentence dictation

Proficiency was achieved for rhyming, beginning sounds, blending onsets and rhymes, concepts of print, and letter naming. Teachers who used the *Beginning Reading Through Speech* approach in their extended day reading program stated that it helped their students make significant gains (Gerber & Klein, 2004). Please refer to Gerber and Klein (2004) for more details about this study.

Unit 1

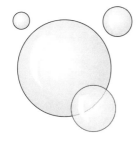

Bubble Sound /b/ → Bb
Pages 3–22

Frisky Cat Sound /f/ → Ff
Pages 23–42

Humming Sound /m/ → Mm
Pages 43–62

Time Sound /t/ → Tt
Pages 63–82

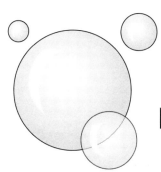

Bubble Sound /b/
Introducing the Bubble Sound /b/

Introduce the **Bubble Sound /b/** by reading the script below to the student(s). Demonstrate and discuss the formation of the **Bubble Sound /b/** (see *Resource Book 2*, Appendix A for a description of the **Bubble Sound /b/**).

Say: *Today we are going to learn about the **Bubble Sound /b/**. Watch me say the **Bubble Sound**: **/b/** (pause) **/b/** (pause) **/b/**. Now it's your turn to make the **Bubble Sound /b/**.*

Have the student(s) practice the **Bubble Sound /b/** aloud. Then, ask the questions in the table below.

Lips	*What are your lips doing when you say the **Bubble Sound /b/**?*
Tongue	*Do you use your tongue to say the **Bubble Sound /b/**?*
Breath	*Is there a burst of air or a long flow of air when you say the **Bubble Sound /b/**?*
Voice	*Feel your neck when you say the **Bubble Sound /b/**. Can you feel any vibration? This is called voice. The **Bubble Sound /b/** has voice.*

Have the student(s) cut out the Picture Symbol Flashcard on page 4. Student(s) can refer to this picture symbol for reinforcement during the Auditory Bombardment Story and throughout the first part of the chapter (Worksheets 1–3).

Note: You will be prompted to create the Letter Flashcard with Worksheet 4.

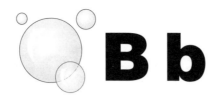 # B b

Picture Symbol Flashcard

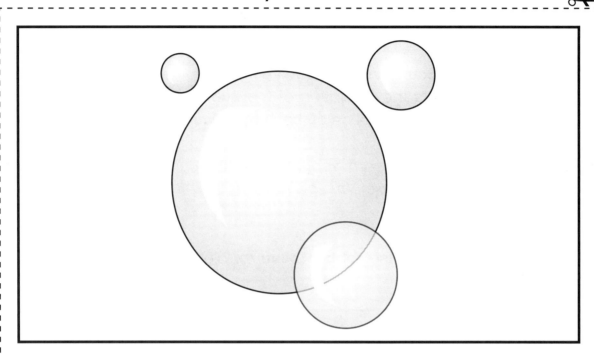

Letter Flashcard

/b/ Flashcards

#BKCD-407 Webber® Hear It! Say It! Learn It!™ • ©2008 Super Duper® Publications • www.superduperinc.com • 1-800-277-8737

Bubble Sound /b/
Auditory Bombardment Story

Directions: Read the story aloud to the student(s) or play it from the CD-ROM.

 Note: You have the option of having "No Text" (for auditory bombardment) or "Text" (for letter/word recognition and reading).

Bobby's Bubbly Boat

Bobby **B**arrett was a **b**oy who loved **b**oats. **B**efore **b**edtime each night, he would play with his favorite **b**oat in the **b**athtub. The **b**oat was a small **b**lack **b**arge that **b**lew **b**ubbles and **b**obbed along in the **b**ath water. The **b**est part of all was that the **b**ubbles made the sound *b*, *b*, *b*.

One night during **B**obby's **b**ath, as his **b**arge **b**obbed along in the **b**athtub, the **b**ubbles suddenly stopped, and there was no more *b*, *b*, *b* sound. **B**obby's **b**arge was **b**roken. **B**obby **b**urst into tears. **B**obby's mom, **B**renda, told him that tomorrow they would go to **B**ailey's Toy **B**arn and **b**uy a new **b**oat.

At **B**ailey's Toy **B**arn, **B**obby **b**egan searching for a new **b**oat. There were **b**arges and rowboats and ships and sailboats. Some were **b**ig, some were **b**umpy, some were **b**izarre, and some were drab. **B**ut none of the **b**oats **b**lew **b**ubbles that made a *b*, *b*, *b* sound. **B**obby **b**egan to **b**elieve he would never find another **b**oat like the **b**lack **b**arge.

Just then, **B**ailey **b**rought out a **b**rand new submarine from the **b**ack of the store. It was a **b**eautiful, **b**right **b**lue submarine that could **b**low **b**igger **b**ubbles and make a louder *b*, *b*, *b* sound than the **b**lack **b**arge ever could. **B**efore **B**obby **B**arrett went to **b**ed that night, he and his **b**right **b**lue submarine had the **b**est **b**ath time ever.

/b/ Auditory Bombardment

Bubble Sound /b/ in Isolation

Directions: Give each student a copy of the **Bubble Sound /b/ Worksheet 1**.

Say: *I'm going to say some sounds, one at a time. If you hear the **Bubble Sound /b/**, put a check mark (✔) on the ball. If you hear a different sound, put an X on the ball. Ready? Number 1, /b/, Number 2, /b/, Number 3, /f/, etc.*

Use additional blank copies of **Worksheet 1** for the sound stimuli in Trial 2 and Trial 3 below. To record data for two or more students, see *Book 2, Appendix B*.

 For more practice, choose the **Bubble Sound /b/** and complete the **Isolation** activity.

	Trial 1		Trial 2		Trial 3	
	Stimulus Sound	**Check if Correct** ✓	**Stimulus Sound**	**Check if Correct** ✓	**Stimulus Sound**	**Check if Correct** ✓
1.	/b/		/b/		/r/	
2.	/b/		/t/		/m/	
3.	/f/		/b/		/b/	
4.	/b/		/b/		/k/	
5.	/s/		/n/		/b/	
6.	/g/		/b/		/v/	
7.	/d/		/p/		/b/	
8.	/b/		/k/		/n/	
9.	/m/		/b/		/p/	
10.	/b/		/f/		/b/	
	Total:		**Total:**		**Total:**	

_____   _____

Student's Name   Date

Scoresheet 1 /b/ in Isolation

#BKCD-407 Webber® Hear It! Say It! Learn It!™ • ©2008 Super Duper® Publications • www.superduperinc.com • 1-800-277-8737

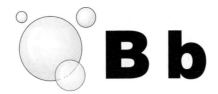
B b

①

②

③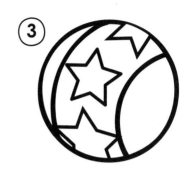

④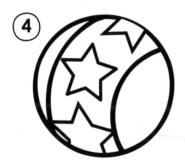

⑤

⑥

⑦

⑧

⑨

⑩

Name _____   Date _____

Bubble Sound /b/ in Syllables

Directions: Give each student a copy of the **Bubble Sound /b/ Worksheet 2**.

Say: *I'm going to say some silly words to you, one at a time. If you hear the **Bubble Sound /b/** in the silly word, circle the bicycle. If you hear a different sound, put an X on the bicycle. Ready? Number 1, bo-bo, Number 2, lo-lo, Number 3, so-so, etc.*

Use additional blank copies of **Worksheet 2** for the sound stimuli in Trial 2 and Trial 3 below. To record data for two or more students, see *Book 2, Appendix B*.

 For more practice, choose the **Bubble Sound /b/** and complete the **Syllables** activity.

	Trial 1		**Trial 2**		**Trial 3**	
	Stimulus Sound	Check if Correct ✓	Stimulus Sound	Check if Correct ✓	Stimulus Sound	Check if Correct ✓
1.	**b**o-**b**o		va-va		**b**ee-**b**ee	
2.	lo-lo		**b**o-**b**o		da-da	
3.	so-so		**b**a-**b**a		lo-lo	
4.	**b**o-**b**o		mo-mo		**b**o-**b**o	
5.	**b**o-**b**o		so-so		moo-moo	
6.	fo-fo		wa-wa		**b**o-**b**o	
7.	ko-ko		fa-fa		na-na	
8.	**b**o-**b**o		**b**a-**b**a		**b**a-**b**a	
9.	po-po		lo-lo		lee-lee	
10.	mo-mo		ma-ma		pa-pa	
	Total:		**Total:**		**Total:**	

_____   _____
Student's Name   Date

Scoresheet 2 /b/ in Syllables

#BKCD-407 Webber® Hear It! Say It! Learn It!™ • ©2008 Super Duper® Publications • www.superduperinc.com • 1-800-277-8737

B b

1

2

3

4

5

6

7

8

9

10

_____   _____

Name   Date

Worksheet 2
/b/ in Syllables

Bubble Sound /b/ in Pictures

Directions: Give each student a copy of the **Bubble Sound /b/ Worksheet 3**.

Say: *I'm going to say some words to you. Listen to me say two words each time. If you hear the **Bubble Sound /b/** at the beginning of the word, circle the picture that begins with the **Bubble Sound /b/**. Ready? Number 1, house - bike, Number 2, ball - face, Number 3, milk - bee, etc.*

To record data for two or more students, see *Book 2, Appendix B*.

 For more practice, choose the **Bubble Sound /b/** and complete the **Pictures** activity.

	Word Pair		Check if Correct ✓
1.	house	**b**ike	
2.	**b**all	face	
3.	milk	**b**ee	
4.	leaf	**b**oy	
5.	**b**eads	chair	
6.	**b**oat	fish	
7.	car	**b**one	
8.	pig	**b**oot	
9.	**b**arn	doll	
10.	sock	**b**ell	
		Total:	

_____   _____
Student's Name   Date

Scoresheet 3 /b/ in Pictures

#BKCD-407 Webber® Hear It! Say It! Learn It!™ • ©2008 Super Duper® Publications • www.superduperinc.com • 1-800-277-8737

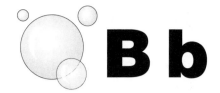

B b

Learning to Write the Letter Bb

Directions: Introduce the letter **Bb**. Have the student(s) cut out the Letter Flashcard from page 4 and glue or tape the backs of the two flashcards (Picture Symbol and Letter) together. Now, student(s) can refer to **both** sides of the flashcard for reinforcement during the remainder of the chapter.

Say: *This is the letter **Bb**. This (point) is the uppercase **B**. This is the lowercase **b**. The letter **Bb** makes the **Bubble Sound /b/**. What is the Bubble Sound?*

Have the student(s) practice forming uppercase **B** and lowercase **b** using the index finger of his/her dominant hand to trace the letters on the flashcards. Demonstrate the action first.

Say: *To make an uppercase **B**, put your finger at the top of the letter. Make a straight line down, like a stick. Pick up your finger and put it back at the top. Make two bubbles attached to the stick.*

*To make a lowercase **b**, put your finger at the top of the letter. Make a straight line down, like a stick. Make a small bubble attached to the stick.*

Note: You may need to modify letter formation and/or verbal cues to best fit with your school's curriculum. For a quick guide to handwriting cues, refer to *Book 2, Appendix C*.

Give each student a copy of the **Bubble Sound /b/ Worksheet 4**. Student(s) will practice writing uppercase **B** and lowercase **b** with a pencil. First, have the student(s) trace within the outlines. Then, trace along the dotted lines. Finally, have the student(s) practice writing the letter without a guide.

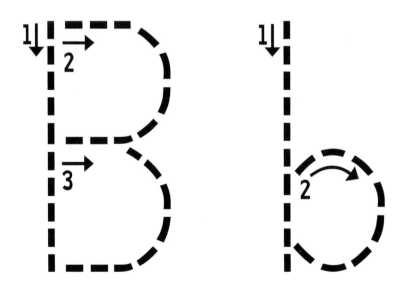

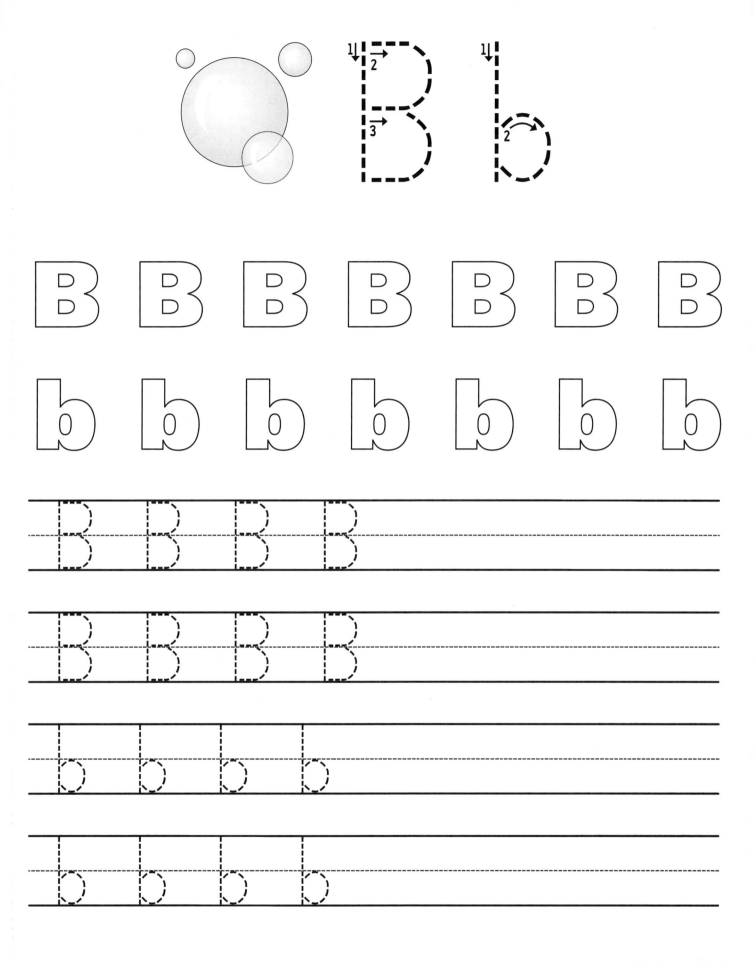

#BKCD-407 Webber® Hear It! Say It! Learn It!™ • ©2008 Super Duper® Publications • www.superduperinc.com • 1-800-277-8737

Bubble Sound /b/ and Letter Bb in Pictures with Initial Letter

Directions: Give each student a copy of the **Bubble Sound /b/ Worksheet 5**.

Say: *I'm going to say some words. Listen to me say two words each time. If you hear the* **Bubble Sound /b/** *at the beginning of the word <u>and</u> see the letter* **Bb**, *circle the picture and letter that begins with the* **Bubble Sound /b/**. *Ready? Number 1, ball - car, Number 2, boy - fan, Number 3, sun - bear, etc.*

To record data for two or more students, see *Book 2, Appendix B*.

 For more practice, choose the **Bubble Sound /b/** and complete the **Pictures & Letters** activity.

	Word Pair		Check if Correct ✓
1.	**b**all	car	
2.	**B**oy	Fan	
3.	sun	**b**ear	
4.	hat	**b**ug	
5.	**B**ell	Dog	
6.	Pig	**B**at	
7.	**b**ed	girl	
8.	**B**oat	Toy	
9.	rake	**b**ee	
10.	**B**oot	Van	
		Total:	

_____   _____
Student's Name   Date

#BKCD-407 Webber® Hear It! Say It! Learn It!™ • ©2008 Super Duper® Publications • www.superduperinc.com • 1-800-277-8737

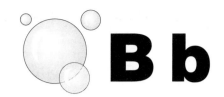

B b

1.	⬤	b		🚗	c
2.	👦	B		🌀	F
3.	☀	s		🐻	b
4.	👒	h		🐜	b
5.	🔔	B		🐕	D
6.	🐖	P		🏏	B
7.	🛏	b		👧	g
8.	🚢	B		🐘	T
9.	🧹	r		🐝	b
10.	👢	B		🚐	V

_____   _____

Name   Date

Practice Writing the Letter Bb

Directions: Give each student a copy of the **Bubble Sound /b/ Worksheet 6**.

Say: *I'm going to say some sounds, one at a time. If you hear the **Bubble Sound /b/**, write an uppercase **B** on the balloon. If you hear a different sound, put an X on the balloon. Ready? Balloon Number 1, /b/, Number 2, /b/, Number 3, /f/, etc.*

Practice writing a lowercase **b** using Trial 2 stimuli on an additional copy of **Worksheet 6**. To record data for two or more students, see *Book 2, Appendix B*.

	Trial 1			Trial 2		
	Stimulus Sound	**Correctly Identified /b/ Sound**	**Correctly Wrote Uppercase B**	**Stimulus Sound**	**Correctly Identified /b/ Sound**	**Correctly Wrote Lowercase b**
1.	**/b/**			/r/		
2.	**/b/**			/m/		
3.	/f/			**/b/**		
4.	**/b/**			/k/		
5.	/s/			**/b/**		
6.	/g/			/v/		
7.	**/b/**			**/b/**		
8.	/m/			/n/		
9.	/p/			**/b/**		
10.	**/b/**			/d/		
	Total:			**Total:**		

_____   _____

Student's Name   Date

#BKCD-407 Webber® Hear It! Say It! Learn It!™ • ©2008 Super Duper® Publications • www.superduperinc.com • 1-800-277-8737

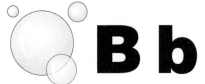

B b

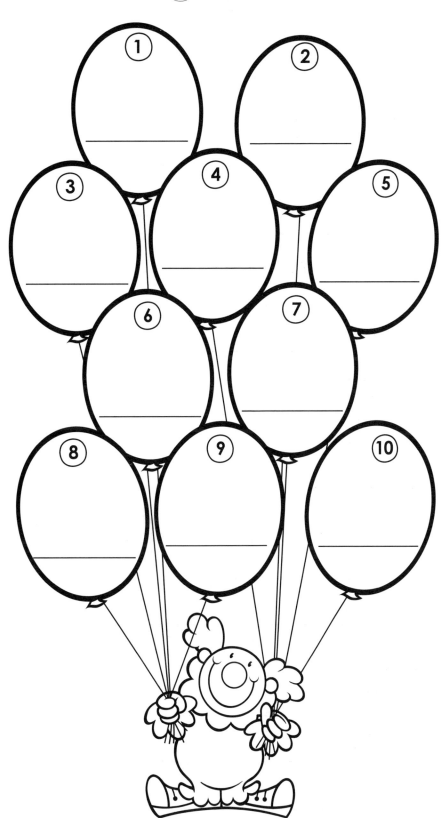

Bubble Sound /b/ and Letter Bb in Pictures and Words

Directions: Give each student a copy of the **Bubble Sound /b/ Worksheet 7**.

Say: *On this paper, we see pictures with words beside them. Look at the pictures and words on the first row. Say the word that names each picture. If the word starts with the* **Bubble Sound /b/** <u>and</u> *you see the letter* **Bb**, *put a circle on that picture. Ready? Number 1, ball - wall, Number 2, pear - bear, Number 3, bee - lee, etc.*

To record data for two or more students, see *Book 2, Appendix B*.

 For more practice, choose the **Bubble Sound /b/** and complete the **Pictures & Words** activity.

	Word Pair		Check if Correct ✓
1.	**b**all	wall	
2.	Pear	**B**ear	
3.	**B**ee	Lee	
4.	**b**oat	coat	
5.	**B**oy	Toy	
6.	hat	**b**at	
7.	**b**ag	rag	
8.	kite	**b**ite	
9.	**b**ell	well	
10.	Rug	**B**ug	
		Total:	

_____   _____
Student's Name   Date

Scoresheet 7
/b/ Pictures
and Words

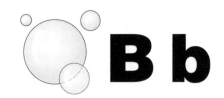

B b

1.		**b**all		wall
2.		Pear		**B**ear
3.		**B**ee		Lee
4.		**b**oat		coat
5.		**B**oy		Toy
6.		hat		**b**at
7.		**b**ag		rag
8.		kite		**b**ite
9.		**b**ell		well
10.		Rug		**B**ug

_____   _____
Name   Date

Bubble Sound /b/ and the Letter Bb in Words

Directions: Give each student a copy of the **Bubble Sound /b/ Worksheet 8**.

Say: *On this paper, we see a list of words. Some of them begin with the letter **Bb** which makes the **Bubble Sound /b/**. I'm going to say two words each time. Point to each word as I say it. Circle the word that begins with the letter **Bb** and the **Bubble Sound /b/**. Ready? Number 1, boy - toy, Number 2, bell - fell, Number 3, hat - bat, etc.*

To record data for two or more students, see *Book 2, Appendix B*.

 For more practice, choose the **Bubble Sound /b/** and complete the **Words** activity.

	Word Pair		Check if Correct ✓
1.	**b**oy	toy	
2.	**B**ell	Fell	
3.	hat	**b**at	
4.	call	**b**all	
5.	tack	**b**ack	
6.	**b**ike	like	
7.	**B**ook	Hook	
8.	Yarn	**B**arn	
9.	**b**ud	mud	
10.	**b**oot	root	
		Total:	

_____   _____

#BKCD-407 Webber® Hear It! Say It! Learn It!™ • ©2008 Super Duper® Publications • www.superduperinc.com • 1-800-277-8737

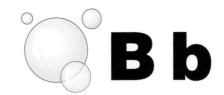

B b

1.	boy	toy
2.	Bell	Fell
3.	hat	bat
4.	call	ball
5.	tack	back
6.	bike	like
7.	Book	Hook
8.	Yarn	Barn
9.	bud	mud
10.	boot	root

_____   _____
Name   Date

Extension Activity for the Bubble Sound /b/

Divide the class into two lines facing each other. Have the first student in one of the lines bounce a ball to the first student in the other line. That student then bounces the ball to the second student in the original line. Continue this pattern to the end of the line. You may continue the activity beginning at the back of the line and move toward the front of the line.

After completing the activity, gather the class around a story chart or chalkboard. Ask the students to tell you about the activity. Write their comments on the chart/board. Then read the sentences together. You should not expect the students to be able to read the story, but they will begin to connect fluent speech with written text and recognize words beginning with the target sound.

Lead the students through a retelling of the activity in the following manner:

1. If possible, use a tape recorder to record the students' sentences about the activity.

2. Replay the taped sentences and write them on the board.

3. After writing each sentence, read each sentence once.

4. Have the class "read" the sentences a second time along with you.

5. As the students read the sentences aloud, move a pointer (or your finger) in a continuous, fluid motion across the words.

6. Encourage the students to come up one by one and point to any words that begin with the target sound and letter (**Bubble Sound /b/**).

See example sentences for this activity below.

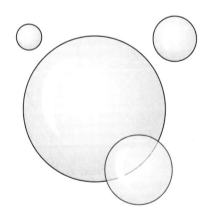

"We played **ball**."

"The **boys bounced** the **ball**."

"The girls **bounced** the **ball**."

"The **ball** was **big**."

Create your own activity and story using the **Bubble Sound /b/**!

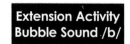

#BKCD-407 Webber® Hear It! Say It! Learn It!™ • ©2008 Super Duper® Publications • www.superduperinc.com • 1-800-277-8737

Frisky Cat Sound /f/
Introducing the Frisky Cat Sound /f/

Introduce the **Frisky Cat Sound /f/** by reading the script below to the student(s). Demonstrate and discuss the formation of the **Frisky Cat Sound /f/** (see *Resource Book 2*, Appendix A for a description of the **Frisky Cat Sound /f/**).

Say: *Today we are going to learn about the **Frisky Cat Sound /f/**. Watch me say the **Frisky Cat Sound**: /f/ (pause) /f/ (pause) /f/. Now it's your turn to make the **Frisky Cat Sound /f/**.*

Have the student(s) practice the **Frisky Cat Sound /f/** aloud. Then, ask the questions in the table below.

Lips	What are your lips doing when you say the **Frisky Cat Sound /f/**?
Tongue	Do you use your tongue to say the **Frisky Cat Sound /f/**?
Breath	Is there a burst of air or a long flow of air when you say the **Frisky Cat Sound /f/**?
Voice	Feel your neck when you say the **Frisky Cat Sound /f/**. Can you feel any vibration? That is because the **Frisky Cat Sound /f/** does not have voice.

Have the student(s) cut out the Picture Symbol Flashcard on page 24. Student(s) can refer to this picture symbol for reinforcement during the Auditory Bombardment Story and throughout the first part of the chapter (Worksheets 1–3).

Note: You will be prompted to create the Letter Flashcard with Worksheet 4.

/f/ Introduction

 # F f

Picture Symbol Flashcard ✂

Letter Flashcard ✂

 #BKCD-407 Webber® Hear It! Say It! Learn It!™ • ©2008 Super Duper® Publications • www.superduperinc.com • 1-800-277-8737

Frisky Cat Sound /f/
Auditory Bombardment Story

Directions: Read the story aloud to the student(s) or play it from the CD-ROM.

Note: You have the option of having "No Text" (for auditory bombardment) or "Text" (for letter/word recognition and reading).

Felicia's Frisky Feline

Felicia **F**oster was a **f**eisty little girl who had a **f**risky cat named **F**iona. **F**iona loved **F**elicia and would **f**ollow her around everywhere she went. **F**iona would carry around her **f**avorite toy—a **f**urry little mouse—hoping **F**elicia would want to play **f**etch. **F**elicia was **f**ar too busy to play. When **F**iona dropped the toy mouse at her **f**eet, **F**elicia would just **f**ling the toy back to **F**iona.

One day, **F**elicia **F**oster was trying to **f**ind her **f**avorite **f**ingernail polish when she tripped over **F**iona's **f**urry little toy mouse. **F**elicia became **f**rustrated and said, "**F**iona, you are in my way. Take your **f**urry little toy and go back to the sofa." **F**iona **f**lipped over on her back and **f**ussed, "***f, f, f.***"

Felicia's **f**ather, Mr. **F**oster, came into her room to **f**ind out what the **f**uss was all about. **F**elicia complained, "**F**iona is **f**ollowing me around and always under my **f**eet. I do not have enough time to play **f**etch. I'm busy with other stuff." Again, **F**iona huffed, "***f, f, f.***" Mr. **F**oster thought about it **f**or a minute, and **f**igured out why **F**iona was saying, "***f, f, f.***" He told **F**elicia, "**F**iona is a **f**riendly cat who is **f**risky and wants your attention. She **f**ollows you because she loves you so much. Don't you think you can **f**ind a **f**ew minutes to play **f**etch with **F**iona?"

Felicia **f**elt sorry **f**or her **f**urry little **f**riend, and she lifted **F**iona into her arms. She had **f**orgotten how soft **F**iona's **f**ur was. **F**elicia promised to **f**ind time **f**or **f**etch, and **F**iona no longer **f**ussed, "***f, f, f.***"

/f/ Auditory Bombardment

Frisky Cat Sound /f/ in Isolation

Directions: Give each student a copy of the **Frisky Cat Sound /f/ Worksheet 1**.

Say: *I'm going to say some sounds, one at a time. If you hear the **Frisky Cat Sound /f/**, put a check mark (✓) on the feet. If you hear a different sound, put an X on the feet. Ready? Number 1, /f/, Number 2, /f/, Number 3, /t/, etc.*

Use additional blank copies of **Worksheet 1** for the sound stimuli in Trial 2 and Trial 3 below. To record data for two or more students, see *Book 2, Appendix B*.

 For more practice, choose the **Frisky Cat Sound /f/** and complete the **Isolation** activity.

	Trial 1		Trial 2		Trial 3	
	Stimulus Sound	**Check if Correct** ✓	**Stimulus Sound**	**Check if Correct** ✓	**Stimulus Sound**	**Check if Correct** ✓
1.	/f/		/f/		/s/	
2.	/f/		/t/		/p/	
3.	/t/		/p/		/f/	
4.	/m/		/g/		/f/	
5.	/f/		/f/		/v/	
6.	/k/		/n/		/m/	
7.	/d/		/f/		/f/	
8.	/w/		/m/		/v/	
9.	/f/		/f/		/s/	
10.	/f/		/s/		/f/	
	Total:		**Total:**		**Total:**	

_____   _____
Student's Name   Date

**Scoresheet 1
/f/ in Isolation**

#BKCD-407 Webber® Hear It! Say It! Learn It!™ • ©2008 Super Duper® Publications • www.superduperinc.com • 1-800-277-8737

 **F f**

① 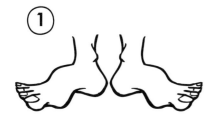   ② 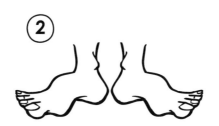   ③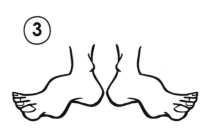

④ 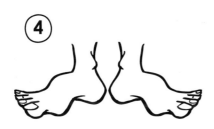   ⑤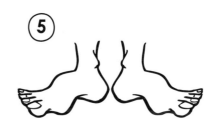

⑥ 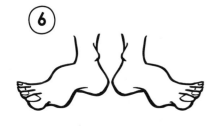   ⑦ 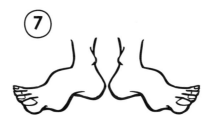   ⑧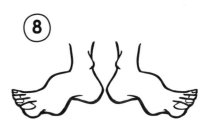

⑨ 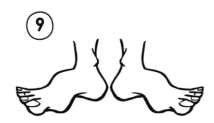   ⑩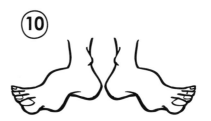

_____   _____

Name   Date

Worksheet 1
/f/ in Isolation

Frisky Cat Sound /f/ in Syllables

Directions: Give each student a copy of the **Frisky Cat Sound /f/ Worksheet 2**.

Say: *I'm going to say some silly words to you, one at a time. If you hear the **Frisky Cat Sound** /f/ in the silly word, circle the fishbowl. If you hear a different sound, put an X on the fish bowl. Ready? Number 1, bo-bo, Number 2, fo-fo, Number 3, lo-lo, etc.*

Use additional blank copies of **Worksheet 2** for the sound stimuli in Trial 2 and Trial 3 below. To record data for two or more students, see *Book 2, Appendix B*.

 For more practice, choose the **Frisky Cat Sound /f/** and complete the **Syllables** activity.

	Trial 1 Stimulus Sound	Trial 1 Check if Correct ✓	Trial 2 Stimulus Sound	Trial 2 Check if Correct ✓	Trial 3 Stimulus Sound	Trial 3 Check if Correct ✓
1.	bo-bo		fa-fa		foo-foo	
2.	fo-fo		lo-lo		da-da	
3.	lo-lo		to-to		lo-lo	
4.	fo-fo		sa-sa		fee-fee	
5.	do-do		fo-fo		soo-soo	
6.	mo-mo		mo-mo		foo-foo	
7.	fo-fo		to-to		va-va	
8.	fo-fo		fa-fa		fa-fa	
9.	go-go		fo-fo		mee-mee	
10.	fo-fo		na-na		ko-ko	
	Total:		Total:		Total:	

_____ _____

Student's Name Date

Scoresheet 2 /f/ in Syllables

#BKCD-407 Webber® Hear It! Say It! Learn It!™ • ©2008 Super Duper® Publications • www.superduperinc.com • 1-800-277-8737

(1)

(2)

(3)

(4)

(5)

(6)

(7)

(8)

(9)

(10)

_____   _____
Name   Date

Worksheet 2
/f/ in Syllables

Frisky Cat Sound /f/ in Pictures

Directions: Give each student a copy of the **Frisky Cat Sound /f/ Worksheet 3**.

Say: *I'm going to say some words to you. Listen to me say two words each time. If you hear the **Frisky Cat Sound /f/** at the beginning of the word, circle the picture that begins with the **Frisky Cat Sound /f/**. Ready? Number 1, foot - hat, Number 2, rope - fair, Number 3, lamp - fork, etc.*

To record data for two or more students, see *Book 2, Appendix B*.

 For more practice, choose the **Frisky Cat Sound /f/** and complete the **Pictures** activity.

	Word Pair		Check if Correct ✓
1.	foot	hat	
2.	rope	fair	
3.	lamp	fork	
4.	fire	horse	
5.	fan	rake	
6.	farm	book	
7.	moon	fast	
8.	soup	five	
9.	food	goat	
10.	bus	fish	
		Total:	

_____   _____
Student's Name   Date

Scoresheet 3 /f/ in Pictures

      #BKCD-407 Webber® Hear It! Say It! Learn It!™ • ©2008 Super Duper® Publications • www.superduperinc.com • 1-800-277-8737

F f

Learning to Write the Letter Ff

Directions: Introduce the letter **Ff**. Have the student(s) cut out the Letter Flashcard from page 24 and glue or tape the backs of the two flashcards (Picture Symbol and Letter) together. Now, student(s) can refer to **both** sides of the flashcard for reinforcement during the remainder of the chapter.

Say: *This is the letter **Ff**. This (point) is the uppercase **F**. This is the lowercase **f**. The letter **Ff** makes the **Frisky Cat Sound /f/**. What is the Frisky Cat Sound?*

Have the student(s) practice forming uppercase **F** and lowercase **f** using the index finger of his/her dominant hand to trace the letters on the flashcards. Demonstrate the action first.

Say: *To make an uppercase **F**, put your finger at the top of the letter. Make a straight line down, like a stick. Pick up your finger and put it back at the top. Make a short line to the side. Make a shorter line to the side at the middle.*

*To make a lowercase **f**, put your finger at the top of the letter. Make a line with a cane at the top. Make a short line across the middle.*

Note: You may need to modify letter formation and/or verbal cues to best fit with your school's curriculum. For a quick guide to handwriting cues, refer to *Book 2, Appendix C*.

Give each student a copy of the **Frisky Cat Sound /f/ Worksheet 4**. Student(s) will practice writing uppercase **F** and lowercase **f** with a pencil. First, have the student(s) trace within the outlines. Then, trace along the dotted lines. Finally, have the student(s) practice writing the letter without a guide.

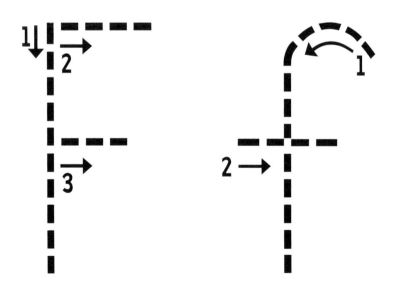

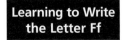

#BKCD-407 Webber® Hear It! Say It! Learn It!™ • ©2008 Super Duper® Publications • www.superduperinc.com • 1-800-277-8737

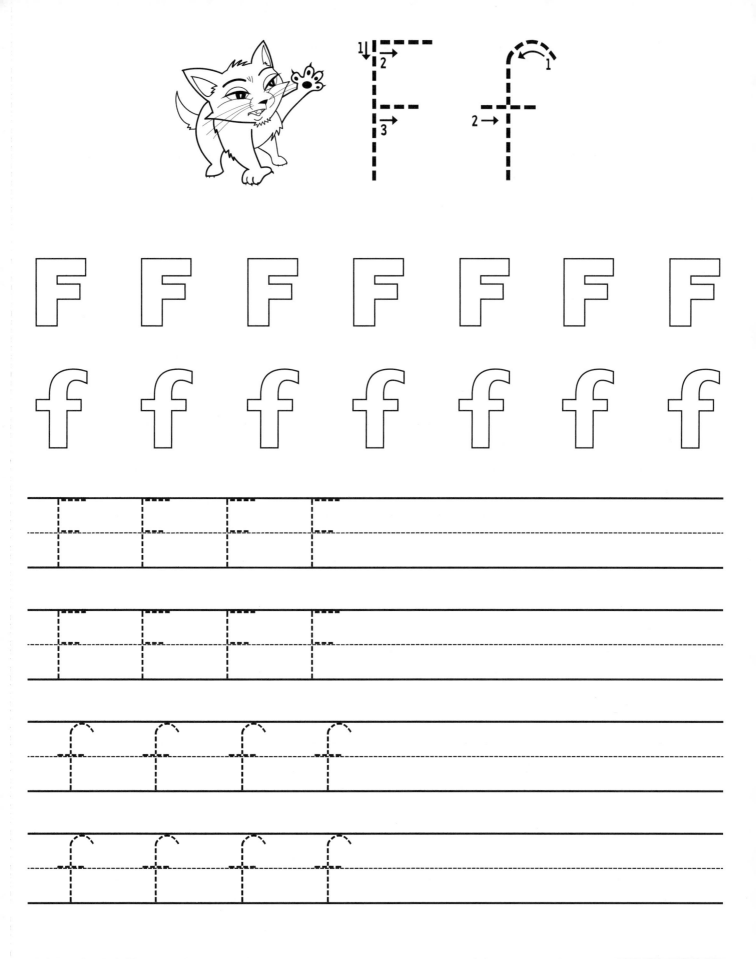

Name

Date

#BKCD-407 Webber® Hear It! Say It! Learn It!™ • ©2008 Super Duper® Publications • www.superduperinc.com • 1-800-277-8737

Frisky Cat Sound /f/ and Letter Ff in Pictures with Initial Letter

Directions: Give each student a copy of the **Frisky Cat Sound /f/ Worksheet 5.**

Say: *I'm going to say some words. Listen to me say two words each time. If you hear the* **Frisky Cat Sound /f/** *at the beginning of the word <u>and</u> see the letter* **Ff***, circle the picture and letter that begins with the* **Frisky Cat Sound /f/***. Ready? Number 1, foot - bug, Number 2, tail - fish, Number 3, fan - cap, etc.*

To record data for two or more students, see *Book 2, Appendix B.*

 For more practice, choose the **Frisky Cat Sound /f/** and complete the **Pictures & Letters** activity.

Word Pair			Check if Correct ✓
1.	foot	bug	
2.	tail	fish	
3.	Fan	Cap	
4.	four	lid	
5.	Ball	Fork	
6.	Fence	Kite	
7.	horn	full	
8.	Lamp	Five	
9.	fire	door	
10.	hive	fall	
		Total:	

_____   _____
Student's Name   Date

**Scoresheet 5
/f/ in Pictures**

#BKCD-407 Webber® Hear It! Say It! Learn It!™ • ©2008 Super Duper® Publications • www.superduperinc.com • 1-800-277-8737

 **F f**

1.		f			b
2.		t			f
3.		F			C
4.	**4**	f			l
5.		B			F
6.		F			K
7.		h			f
8.		L		**5**	F
9.		f			d
10.		h			f

_____
Name

_____
Date

#BKCD-407 Webber® Hear It! Say It! Learn It!™ • ©2008 Super Duper® Publications • www.superduperinc.com • 1-800-277-8737

Practice Writing the Letter Ff

Directions: Give each student a copy of the **Frisky Cat Sound /f/ Worksheet 6**.

Say: *I'm going to say some sounds, one at a time. If you hear the **Frisky Cat Sound /f/**, write an uppercase **F** on the feather. If you hear a different sound, put an X on the feather. Ready? Feather Number 1, /f/, Number 2, /p/, Number 3, /f/, etc.*

Practice writing a lowercase **f** using Trial 2 stimuli on an additional copy of **Worksheet 6**. To record data for two or more students, see *Book 2, Appendix B*.

	Trial 1			Trial 2		
	Stimulus Sound	Correctly Identified /f/ Sound	Correctly Wrote Uppercase F	Stimulus Sound	Correctly Identified /f/ Sound	Correctly Wrote Lowercase f
1.	/f/			/v/		
2.	/p/			/f/		
3.	/f/			/s/		
4.	/k/			/f/		
5.	/s/			/f/		
6.	/f/			/p/		
7.	/m/			/d/		
8.	/f/			/g/		
9.	/v/			/f/		
10.	/f/			/f/		
	Total:			Total:		

_____   _____

Student's Name   Date

**Scoresheet 6
Writing Ff**

#BKCD-407 Webber® Hear It! Say It! Learn It!™ • ©2008 Super Duper® Publications • www.superduperinc.com • 1-800-277-8737

Trial _____

F f

Frisky Cat Sound /f/ and Letter Ff in Pictures and Words

Directions: Give each student a copy of the **Frisky Cat Sound /f/ Worksheet 7**.

Say: *On this paper, we see pictures with words beside them. Look at the pictures and words on the first row. Say the word that names each picture. If the word starts with the* **Frisky Cat Sound /f/** <u>and</u> *you see the letter* **Ff***, put a circle on that picture. Ready? Number 1, fan - can, Number 2, dish - fish, Number 3, tire - fire, etc.*

To record data for two or more students, see *Book 2, Appendix B*.

 For more practice, choose the **Frisky Cat Sound /f/** and complete the **Pictures & Words** activity.

	Word Pair		Check if Correct ✓
1.	**F**an	Can	
2.	dish	**f**ish	
3.	Tire	**F**ire	
4.	**f**our	pour	
5.	beet	**f**eet	
6.	**f**ace	lace	
7.	**F**all	Ball	
8.	Arm	**F**arm	
9.	**f**ive	hive	
10.	Mix	**F**ix	
		Total:	

_____
Student's Name

_____
Date

#BKCD-407 Webber® Hear It! Say It! Learn It!™ • ©2008 Super Duper® Publications • www.superduperinc.com • 1-800-277-8737

 # F f

1.		**F**an			Can
2.		dish			**f**ish
3.		Tire			**F**ire
4.		**f**our			pour
5.		beet			**f**eet
6.		**f**ace			lace
7.		**F**all			Ball
8.		Arm			**F**arm
9.		**f**ive			hive
10.		Mix			**F**ix

_____   _____
                Name   Date

Frisky Cat Sound /f/ and the Letter Ff in Words

Directions: Give each student a copy of the **Frisky Cat Sound /f/ Worksheet 8**.

Say: *On this paper, we see a list of words. Some of them begin with the letter **Ff** which makes the **Frisky Cat Sound /f/**. I'm going to say two words each time. Point to each word as I say it. Circle the word that begins with the letter **Ff** and the **Frisky Cat Sound /f/**. Ready? Number 1, sit - fit, Number 2, well - fell, Number 3, fed - bed, etc.*

To record data for two or more students, see *Book 2, Appendix B*.

 For more practice, choose the **Frisky Cat Sound /f/** and complete the **Words** activity.

	Word Pair		Check if Correct ✓
1.	sit	**f**it	
2.	well	**f**ell	
3.	**F**ed	Bed	
4.	heel	**f**eel	
5.	Dawn	**F**awn	
6.	**f**oot	soot	
7.	**f**ig	wig	
8.	hog	**f**og	
9.	**F**ort	Port	
10.	**F**old	Cold	
		Total:	

_____   _____
Student's Name   Date

#BKCD-407 Webber® Hear It! Say It! Learn It!™ • ©2008 Super Duper® Publications • www.superduperinc.com • 1-800-277-8737

F f

1.	sit	fit
2.	well	fell
3.	Fed	Bed
4.	heel	feel
5.	Dawn	Fawn
6.	foot	soot
7.	fig	wig
8.	hog	fog
9.	Fort	Port
10.	Fold	Cold

_____   _____
Name   Date

#BKCD-407 Webber® Hear It! Say It! Learn It!™ • ©2008 Super Duper® Publications • www.superduperinc.com • 1-800-277-8737

Extension Activity for Frisky Cat Sound /f/

Print and/or copy and cut out pictures from **Frisky Cat Sound /f/ Worksheet 3**—or another source, such as a magazine—that begin with **/f/**. Hide these pictures around the room. Engage the class in a treasure hunt activity. Clues and hiding place examples are in the chart below.

Hiding Place	Level 1 Clues	Level 2 Clues
On the teacher's desk under an apple	Find a Frisky Cat Sound under the apple on my desk.	Find a Frisky Cat Sound under a red fruit that is on a desk.
On top of a book shelf	Find a Frisky Cat Sound on the (black) bookshelf.	Find a Frisky Cat Sound on a shelf that holds things you read.
On the bulletin board	Find a Frisky Cat Sound on the calendar that is on the bulletin board.	Find a Frisky Cat Sound on something that tells you when it is Friday.
Under the chair	Find a Frisky Cat Sound under a chair.	Find a Frisky Cat Sound under something you sit on.

After completing the activity, gather the class around a story chart or chalkboard. Ask the students to tell you about the activity. Write their comments on the chart/board. Then read the sentences together. You should not expect the students to be able to read the story, but they will begin to connect fluent speech with written text and recognize words beginning with the target sound.

Lead the students through a retelling of the activity in the following manner:

1. If possible, use a tape recorder to record the students' sentences about the activity.
2. Replay the taped sentences and write them on the board.
3. After writing each sentence, read each sentence once.
4. Have the class "read" the sentences a second time along with you.
5. As the students read the sentences aloud, move a pointer (or your finger) in a continuous, fluid motion across the words.
6. Encourage the students to come up one by one and point to any words that begin with the target sound and letter (**Frisky Cat Sound /f/**).

See example sentences for this activity below.

"We **found** a **fish** on the desk."   "The **foot** was stuck to **Friday** on the calendar."

"We **found** a **fork** on the **floor**."   "Megan **found** the **fan** under her chair."

Create your own activity and story using the **Frisky Cat Sound /f/**!

Humming Sound /m/
Introducing the Humming Sound /m/

Introduce the **Humming Sound /m/** by reading the script below to the student(s). Demonstrate and discuss the formation of the **Humming Sound /m/** (see *Resource Book 2, Appendix A* for a description of the **Humming Sound /m/**).

Say: *Today we are going to learn about the **Humming Sound /m/**. Watch me say the **Humming Sound**: /m/ (pause) /m/ (pause) /m/. Now it's your turn to make the **Humming Sound /m/**.*

Have the student(s) practice the **Humming Sound /m/** aloud. Then, ask the questions in the table below.

Lips	*What are your lips doing when you say the **Humming Sound /m/**?*
Tongue	*Do you use your tongue to say the **Humming Sound /m/**?*
Breath	*Is there a burst of air or a long flow of air when you say the **Humming Sound /m/**?*
Voice	*Feel your neck when you say the **Humming Sound /m/**. Can you feel any vibration? This is called voice. The **Humming Sound /m/** has voice.*

Have the student(s) cut out the Picture Symbol Flashcard on page 44. Student(s) can refer to this picture symbol for reinforcement during the Auditory Bombardment Story and throughout the first part of the chapter (Worksheets 1–3).

Note: You will be prompted to create the Letter Flashcard with Worksheet 4.

/m/ Introduction

M m

Picture Symbol Flashcard

Letter Flashcard

/m/ Flashcards

#BKCD-407 Webber® Hear It! Say It! Learn It!™ • ©2008 Super Duper® Publications • www.superduperinc.com • 1-800-277-8737

Humming Sound /m/
Auditory Bombardment Story

Directions: Read the story aloud to the student(s) or play it from the CD-ROM.

Note: You have the option of having "No Text" (for auditory bombardment) or "Text" (for letter/word recognition and reading).

Humming Michael Malone

Michael **M**alone was a small boy who loved to hum. He often hummed, "*m*, *m*, *m*" throughout the day. For someone so small, **M**ichael could hum very loudly. **M**ost people knew when **M**ichael was coming because they could hear him humming, "*m*, *m*, *m*" before they could even see him.

One **M**onday, **M**ichael started humming first thing in the **m**orning, "*m*, *m*, *m*." He hummed on the way to **m**eet the school bus, and he hummed in homeroom, "*m*, *m*, *m*." He even started humming in **m**ath class, but his "*m*, *m*, *m*" **m**ade the other students **m**ad. Finally, his teacher, **M**rs. **M**artin, said, "Michael, **m**ust you always hum?" **M**ichael smiled sheepishly and explained, "Humming helps **m**e with **m**y **m**ath." **M**rs. **M**artin considered this for a **m**inute, "**M**aybe humming could help the rest of **m**y class learn their **m**ath facts." She **m**ade up her **m**ind and told the class to try humming the **m**ath facts. Now, on **m**ost days, you can walk past **M**rs. **M**artin's **m**ath class and hear her class humming, "*m*, *m*, *m*." **M**ichael and his classmates are **m**arvelous at **m**ath!

Humming Sound /m/ in Isolation

Directions: Give each student a copy of the **Humming Sound /m/ Worksheet 1**.

Say: *I'm going to say some sounds, one at a time. If you hear the **Humming Sound /m/**, put a check mark (✓) on the mouse. If you hear a different sound, put an X on the mouse. Ready? Number 1, /m/, Number 2, /m/, Number 3, /s/, etc.*

Use additional blank copies of **Worksheet 1** for the sound stimuli in Trial 2 and Trial 3 below. To record data for two or more students, see *Book 2, Appendix B*.

 For more practice, choose the **Humming Sound /m/** and complete the **Isolation** activity.

	Trial 1		Trial 2		Trial 3	
	Stimulus Sound	**Check if Correct** ✓	**Stimulus Sound**	**Check if Correct** ✓	**Stimulus Sound**	**Check if Correct** ✓
1.	/m/		/m/		/m/	
2.	/m/		/f/		/m/	
3.	/s/		/b/		/k/	
4.	/d/		/m/		/m/	
5.	/m/		/m/		/t/	
6.	/p/		/s/		/b/	
7.	/m/		/n/		/m/	
8.	/l/		/f/		/d/	
9.	/m/		/m/		/n/	
10.	/m/		/m/		/m/	
	Total:		**Total:**		**Total:**	

_____   _____
Student's Name   Date

Scoresheet 1
/m/ in Isolation

#BKCD-407 Webber® Hear It! Say It! Learn It!™ • ©2008 Super Duper® Publications • www.superduperinc.com • 1-800-277-8737

M m

Trial _____

①

②

③

④

⑤

⑥

⑦

⑧

⑨

⑩

Name _____   Date _____

Worksheet 1
/m/ in Isolation

Humming Sound /m/ in Syllables

Directions: Give each student a copy of the **Humming Sound /m/ Worksheet 2**.

Say: *I'm going to say some silly words to you, one at a time. If you hear the **Humming Sound /m/** in the silly word, circle the map. If you hear a different sound, put an X on the map. Ready? Number 1, mo-mo, Number 2, lo-lo, Number 3, so-so, etc.*

Use additional blank copies of **Worksheet 2** for the sound stimuli in Trial 2 and Trial 3 below. To record data for two or more students, see *Book 2, Appendix B*.

 For more practice, choose the **Humming Sound /m/** and complete the **Syllables** activity.

	Trial 1		Trial 2		Trial 3	
	Stimulus Sound	**Check if Correct** ✓	**Stimulus Sound**	**Check if Correct** ✓	**Stimulus Sound**	**Check if Correct** ✓
1.	mo-mo		ma-ma		moo-moo	
2.	lo-lo		fa-fa		mee-mee	
3.	so-so		bo-bo		pa-pa	
4.	mo-mo		la-la		loo-loo	
5.	po-po		mo-mo		da-da	
6.	mo-mo		sa-sa		ma-ma	
7.	mo-mo		wo-wo		mo-mo	
8.	ko-ko		mo-mo		wa-wa	
9.	mo-mo		ma-ma		mee-mee	
10.	mo-mo		po-po		koo-koo	
	Total:		**Total:**		**Total:**	

_____   _____
Student's Name   Date

#BKCD-407 Webber® Hear It! Say It! Learn It!™ • ©2008 Super Duper® Publications • www.superduperinc.com • 1-800-277-8737

Trial _____

M m

①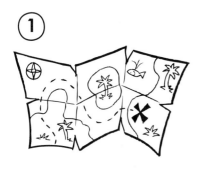

②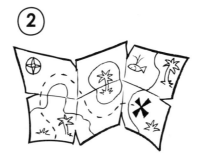

③

④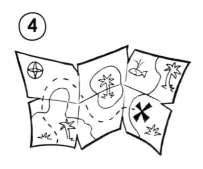

⑤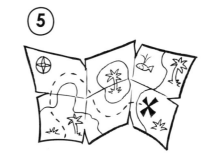

⑥

⑦

⑧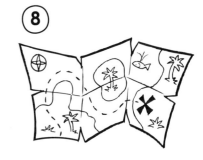

⑨

⑩

_____ _____
Name   Date

Humming Sound /m/ in Pictures

Directions: Give each student a copy of the **Humming Sound /m/ Worksheet 3**.

Say: *I'm going to say some words to you. Listen to me say two words each time. If you hear the* **Humming Sound /m/** *at the beginning of the word, circle the picture that begins with the* **Humming Sound /m/**. *Ready? Number 1, bowl - mouse, Number 2, milk - floor, Number 3, meat - doll, etc.*

To record data for two or more students, see *Book 2, Appendix B*.

  For more practice, choose the **Humming Sound /m/** and complete the **Pictures** activity.

	Word Pair		Check if Correct ✓
1.	bowl	**m**ouse	
2.	**m**ilk	floor	
3.	**m**eat	doll	
4.	corn	**m**outh	
5.	shoe	**m**op	
6.	**m**oose	saw	
7.	**m**ail	nest	
8.	rose	**m**ud	
9.	**m**oon	pie	
10.	cat	**m**ug	
		Total:	

_____   _____

Student's Name   Date

#BKCD-407 Webber® Hear It! Say It! Learn It!™ • ©2008 Super Duper® Publications • www.superduperinc.com • 1-800-277-8737

M m

1.			6.		
2.			7.		
3.			8.		
4.			9.		
5.			10.		

_____   _____

Name   Date

Worksheet 3
/m/ in Pictures

Learning to Write the Letter Mm

Directions: Introduce the letter **Mm**. Have the student(s) cut out the Letter Flashcard from page 44 and glue or tape the backs of the two flashcards (Picture Symbol and Letter) together. Now, student(s) can refer to **both** sides of the flashcard for reinforcement during the remainder of the chapter.

Say: *This is the letter **Mm**. This (point) is the uppercase **M**. This is the lowercase **m**. The letter **Mm** makes the **Humming Sound /m/**. What is the Humming Sound?*

Have the student(s) practice forming uppercase **M** and lowercase **m** using the index finger of his/her dominant hand to trace the letters on the flashcards. Demonstrate the action first.

Say: *To make an uppercase **M**, put your finger at the top of the letter. Make a straight line down, like a stick. Pick up your finger and put it back at the top, next to the first line. Make a slanted line down. Pick up your finger and put it at the top. Make a slanted line down to meet the first slanted line. Pick up your finger and go back to the top. Make a straight line back down to the bottom. (Like making two mountains next to each other.)*

*To make a lowercase **m**, put your finger at the top of the letter. Make a line down to the bottom, like a stick. Pick up your finger and put it back at the top. Make a backward cane attached to the stick. Pick up your finger and put it at the top of the cane. Make another backward cane. (Like making two hills next to each other.)*

Note: You may need to modify letter formation and/or verbal cues to best fit with your school's curriculum. For a quick guide to handwriting cues, refer to *Book 2, Appendix C*.

Give each student a copy of the **Humming Sound /m/ Worksheet 4**. Student(s) will practice writing uppercase **M** and lowercase **m** with a pencil. First, have the student(s) trace within the outlines. Then, trace along the dotted lines. Finally, have the student(s) practice writing the letter without a guide.

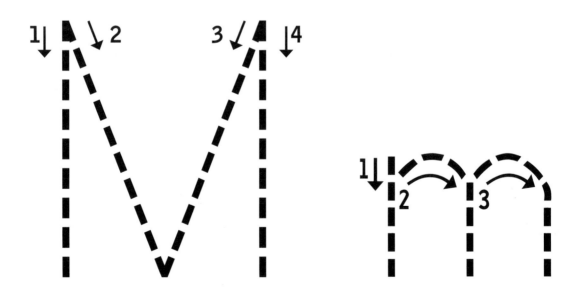

Learning to Write
the Letter Mm

Name

Date

**Worksheet 4
Writing Mm**

Humming Sound /m/ and Letter Mm in Pictures with Initial Letter

Directions: Give each student a copy of the **Humming Sound /m/ Worksheet 5**.

Say: *I'm going to say some words. Listen to me say two words each time. If you hear the* **Humming Sound /m/** *at the beginning of the word <u>and</u> see the letter* **Mm***, circle the picture and letter that begins with the* **Humming Sound /m/***. Ready? Number 1, mail - book, Number 2, goose - mug, Number 3, milk - van, etc.*

To record data for two or more students, see *Book 2, Appendix B*.

 For more practice, choose the **Humming Sound /m/** and complete the **Pictures & Letters** activity.

	Word Pair		Check if Correct ✓
1.	**m**ail	book	
2.	Goose	**M**ug	
3.	**m**ilk	van	
4.	hog	**m**ap	
5.	Nine	**M**ud	
6.	**m**ouse	car	
7.	nest	**m**an	
8.	**M**arch	Dog	
9.	**m**elt	tie	
10.	Pen	**M**ask	
		Total:	

_____   _____
Student's Name   Date

Scoresheet 5
/m/ in Pictures

M m

1.		m		b
2.		G		M
3.		m		v
4.		h		m
5.	**9**	N		M
6.		m		c
7.		n		m
8.		M		D
9.		m		t
10.		P		M

_____   _____
Name   Date

Worksheet 5 /m/ in Pictures

#BKCD-407 Webber® Hear It! Say It! Learn It!™ • ©2008 Super Duper® Publications • www.superduperinc.com • 1-800-277-8737

Practice Writing the Letter Mm

Directions: Give each student a copy of the **Humming Sound /m/ Worksheet 6**.

Say: *I'm going to say some sounds, one at a time. If you hear the **Humming Sound /m/**, write an uppercase **M** on the mushroom. If you hear a different sound, put an X on the mushroom. Ready? Mushroom Number 1, /m/, Number 2, /b/, Number 3, /m/, etc.*

Practice writing a lowercase **m** using Trial 2 stimuli on an additional copy of **Worksheet 6**. To record data for two or more students, see *Book 2, Appendix B*.

	Trial 1			Trial 2		
	Stimulus Sound	**Correctly Identified /m/ Sound**	**Correctly Wrote Uppercase M**	**Stimulus Sound**	**Correctly Identified /m/ Sound**	**Correctly Wrote Lowercase m**
1.	**/m/**			**/m/**		
2.	/b/			**/m/**		
3.	**/m/**			/t/		
4.	/s/			/n/		
5.	/d/			**/m/**		
6.	**/m/**			/l/		
7.	/p/			**/m/**		
8.	**/m/**			**/m/**		
9.	/v/			/s/		
10.	/k/			**/m/**		
	Total:			Total:		

_____   _____
Student's Name   Date

#BKCD-407 Webber® Hear It! Say It! Learn It!™ • ©2008 Super Duper® Publications • www.superduperinc.com • 1-800-277-8737

M m

_____ _____
Name   Date

**Worksheet 6
Writing Mm**

Humming Sound /m/ and Letter Mm in Pictures and Words

Directions: Give each student a copy of the **Humming Sound /m/ Worksheet 7**.

Say: *On this paper, we see pictures with words beside them. Look at the pictures and words on the first row. Say the word that names each picture. If the word starts with the **Humming Sound /m/** <u>and</u> you see the letter **Mm**, put a circle on that picture. Ready? Number 1, man - fan, Number 2, top - mop, Number 3, bud - mud, etc.*

To record data for two or more students, see *Book 2, Appendix B*.

 For more practice, choose the **Humming Sound /m/** and complete the **Pictures & Words** activity.

	Word Pair		Check if Correct ✓
1.	**M**an	Fan	
2.	top	**m**op	
3.	bud	**m**ud	
4.	**m**ice	ice	
5.	**M**ail	Tail	
6.	**m**ap	cap	
7.	Goose	**M**oose	
8.	path	**m**ath	
9.	**M**ug	Bug	
10.	**m**oon	spoon	
		Total:	

_____   _____
Student's Name   Date

Scoresheet 7 /m/ Pictures and Words

   #BKCD-407 Webber® Hear It! Say It! Learn It!™ • ©2008 Super Duper® Publications • www.superduperinc.com • 1-800-277-8737

M m

1.		**M**an		Fan
2.		top		**m**op
3.		bud		**m**ud
4.		**m**ice		ice
5.		**M**ail		Tail
6.		**m**ap		cap
7.		Goose		**M**oose
8.		path		**m**ath
9.		**M**ug		Bug
10.		**m**oon		spoon

_____   _____
Name   Date

Worksheet 7
/m/ in Pictures
and Words

#BKCD-407 *Webber® Hear It! Say It! Learn It!™* • ©2008 Super Duper® Publications • www.superduperinc.com • 1-800-277-8737   59

Humming Sound /m/ and the Letter Mm in Words

Directions: Give each student a copy of the **Humming Sound /m/ Worksheet 8**.

Say: *On this paper, we see a list of words. Some of them begin with the letter **Mm** which makes the **Humming Sound /m/**. I'm going to say two words each time. Point to each word as I say it. Circle the word that begins with the letter **Mm** and the **Humming Sound /m/**. Ready? Number 1, men - ten, Number 2, ball - mall, Number 3, sat - mat, etc.*

To record data for two or more students, see *Book 2, Appendix B*.

 For more practice, choose the **Humming Sound /m/** and complete the **Words** activity.

	Word Pair		Check if Correct ✓
1.	**m**en	ten	
2.	Ball	**M**all	
3.	sat	**m**at	
4.	top	**m**op	
5.	fuss	**m**uss	
6.	**M**ouse	House	
7.	**m**old	gold	
8.	**M**ap	Nap	
9.	Seal	**M**eal	
10.	**m**ail	pail	
		Total:	

_____   _____

Scoresheet 8
/m/ in Words

 #BKCD-407 Webber® Hear It! Say It! Learn It!™ • ©2008 Super Duper® Publications • www.superduperinc.com • 1-800-277-8737

M m

1.	men	ten
2.	Ball	Mall
3.	sat	mat
4.	top	mop
5.	fuss	muss
6.	Mouse	House
7.	mold	gold
8.	Map	Nap
9.	Seal	Meal
10.	mail	pail

_____   _____   **Worksheet 8**
Name   Date   **/m/ in Words**

Extension Activity for the Humming Sound /m/

Give clay or play dough to each student. Brainstorm with the student(s) words that begin with the **Humming Sound /m/.** Write these words on the chalkboard and read them as a group. Then, have the students use the clay to mold objects from this list of words, or any other objects they can think of, that start with the **Humming Sound /m/,** such as "moon."

After completing the activity, gather the class around a story chart or chalkboard. Ask the students to tell you about the activity. Write their comments on the chart/board. Then read the sentences together. You should not expect the students to be able to read the story, but they will begin to connect fluent speech with written text and recognize words beginning with the target sound.

Lead the students through a retelling of the activity in the following manner:

1. If possible, use a tape recorder to record the students' sentences about the activity.

2. Replay the taped sentences and write them on the board.

3. After writing each sentence, read each sentence once.

4. Have the class "read" the sentences a second time along with you.

5. As the students read the sentences aloud, move a pointer (or your finger) in a continuous, fluid motion across the words.

6. Encourage the students to come up one by one and point to any words that begin with the target sound and letter (**Humming Sound /m/**).

See example sentences for this activity below.

"We **made** things with clay."

"I **made** a **moon**."

"I **molded** a **mouse**."

"Clint **molded** a **monkey**."

Create your own activity and story using the **Humming Sound /m/**!

#BKCD-407 Webber® Hear It! Say It! Learn It!™ • ©2008 Super Duper® Publications • www.superduperinc.com • 1-800-277-8737

Time Sound /t/
Introducing the Time Sound /t/

Introduce the **Time Sound /t/** by reading the script below to the student(s). Demonstrate and discuss the formation of the **Time Sound /t/** (see *Resource Book 2, Appendix A* for a description of the **Time Sound /t/**).

Say: *Today we are going to learn about the **Time Sound /t/**. Watch me say the **Time Sound**: /t/ (pause) /t/ (pause) /t/. Now it's your turn to make the **Time Sound /t/**.*

Have the student(s) practice the **Time Sound /t/** aloud. Then, ask the questions in the table below.

Lips	*What are your lips doing when you say the **Time Sound /t/**?*
Tongue	*Do you use your tongue to say the **Time Sound /t/**?*
Breath	*Is there a burst of air or a long flow of air when you say the **Time Sound /t/**?*
Voice	*Feel your neck when you say the **Time Sound /t/**. Can you feel any vibration? That is because the **Time Sound /t/** does not have voice.*

Have the student(s) cut out the Picture Symbol Flashcard on page 64. Student(s) can refer to this picture symbol for reinforcement during the Auditory Bombardment Story and throughout the first part of the chapter (Worksheets 1–3).

Note: You will be prompted to create the Letter Flashcard with Worksheet 4.

/t/ Introduction

Picture Symbol Flashcard

Letter Flashcard

T t

/t/ Flashcards

#BKCD-407 Webber® Hear It! Say It! Learn It!™ • ©2008 Super Duper® Publications • www.superduperinc.com • 1-800-277-8737

Time Sound /t/
Auditory Bombardment Story

Directions: Read the story aloud to the student(s) or play it from the CD-ROM.

Note: You have the option of having "No Text" (for auditory bombardment) or "Text" (for letter/word recognition and reading).

Tommy's Alarm Clock

Tommy **T**urner was a **t**iny little boy who was **t**erribly late for school most of the **t**ime. The alarm clock in **T**ommy's **t**iny room sat next **t**o him on **t**op of his bedside **t**able. **T**ommy went **t**o sleep each night **t**o the **t**icking of the clock—*t*, *t*, *t*.

One night, **T**ommy had a dream. **T**ommy was playing **t**ag with his alarm clock. The clock **t**ried **t**o catch **T**ommy and **t**eased, "*t*, *t*, *t*, it's **t**ime **t**o catch **T**ommy." **T**ommy laughed and **t**ried **t**o run away from the clock. He asked, "Why are you **t**rying **t**o catch me?" The clock said, "**T**o keep you from being **t**erribly late for school **t**omorrow."

The next morning, **T**ommy woke up on **t**ime **t**o the *t*, *t*, *t* of his alarm clock. His mother was delighted **t**o see him downstairs on **t**ime. He even got **t**o school on **t**ime and was never **t**erribly late for school again.

Time Sound /t/ in Isolation

Directions: Give each student a copy of the **Time Sound /t/ Worksheet 1**.

Say: *I'm going to say some sounds, one at a time. If you hear the **Time Sound /t/**, put a check mark (✓) on the table. If you hear a different sound, put an X on the table. Ready? Number 1, /t/, Number 2, /t/, Number 3, /m/, etc.*

Use additional blank copies of **Worksheet 1** for the sound stimuli in Trial 2 and Trial 3 below. To record data for two or more students, see *Book 2, Appendix B.*

 For more practice, choose the **Time Sound /t/** and complete the **Isolation** activity.

	Trial 1		Trial 2		Trial 3	
	Stimulus Sound	**Check if Correct** ✓	**Stimulus Sound**	**Check if Correct** ✓	**Stimulus Sound**	**Check if Correct** ✓
1.	/t/		/t/		/t/	
2.	/t/		/f/		/k/	
3.	/m/		/d/		/t/	
4.	/v/		/t/		/t/	
5.	/t/		/t/		/f/	
6.	/g/		/k/		/m/	
7.	/k/		/m/		/g/	
8.	/t/		/l/		/p/	
9.	/t/		/t/		/t/	
10.	/f/		/t/		/t/	
	Total:		**Total:**		**Total:**	

_____   _____
Student's Name   Date

Scoresheet 1 /t/ in Isolation

#BKCD-407 Webber® Hear It! Say It! Learn It!™ • ©2008 Super Duper® Publications • www.superduperinc.com • 1-800-277-8737

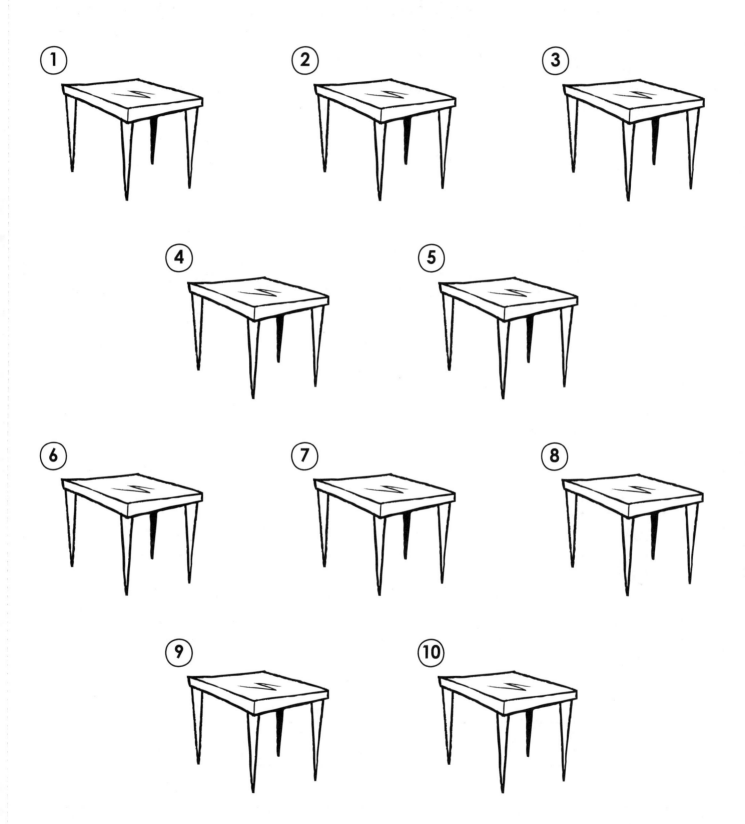

Time Sound /t/ in Syllables

Directions: Give each student a copy of the **Time Sound /t/ Worksheet 2**.

Say: *I'm going to say some silly words to you, one at a time. If you hear the **Time Sound /t/** in the silly word, circle the towel. If you hear a different sound, put an X on the towel. Ready? Number 1, to-to, Number 2, lo-lo, Number 3, go-go, etc.*

Use additional blank copies of **Worksheet 2** for the sound stimuli in Trial 2 and Trial 3 below. To record data for two or more students, see *Book 2, Appendix B.*

 For more practice, choose the **Time Sound /t/** and complete the **Syllables** activity.

	Trial 1		Trial 2		Trial 3	
	Stimulus Sound	Check if Correct ✓	Stimulus Sound	Check if Correct ✓	Stimulus Sound	Check if Correct ✓
1.	to-to		ta-ta		to-to	
2.	lo-lo		to-to		tee-tee	
3.	go-go		ga-ga		ba-ba	
4.	to-to		na-na		do-do	
5.	no-no		to-to		nee-nee	
6.	to-to		da-da		ta-ta	
7.	to-to		ta-ta		too-too	
8.	po-po		no-no		loo-loo	
9.	to-to		pa-pa		to-to	
10.	ko-ko		to-to		tee-tee	
	Total:		Total:		Total:	

_____   _____
Student's Name   Date

#BKCD-407 Webber® Hear It! Say It! Learn It!™ • ©2008 Super Duper® Publications • www.superduperinc.com • 1-800-277-8737

Trial _____

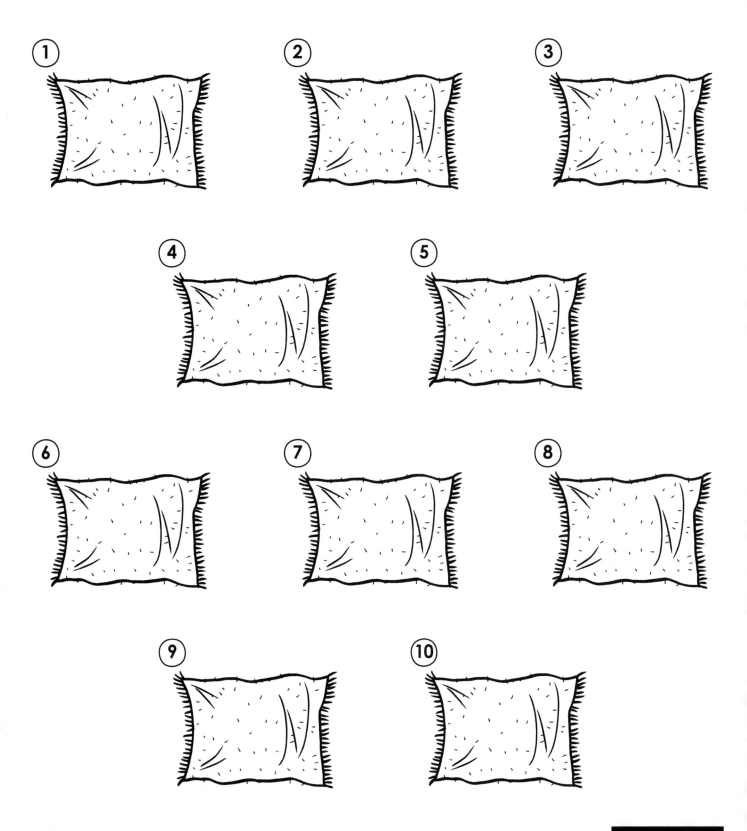

①
②
③
④
⑤
⑥
⑦
⑧
⑨
⑩

_____
Name

_____
Date

Time Sound /t/ in Pictures

Directions: Give each student a copy of the **Time Sound /t/ Worksheet 3**.

Say: *I'm going to say some words to you. Listen to me say two words each time. If you hear the **Time Sound /t/** at the beginning of the word, circle the picture that begins with the **Time Sound /t/**. Ready? Number 1, tail - moon, Number 2, tie - bed, Number 3, soup - tin, etc.*

To record data for two or more students, see *Book 2, Appendix B.*

 For more practice, choose the **Time Sound /t/** and complete the **Pictures** activity.

	Word Pair		Check if Correct ✓
1.	tail	moon	
2.	tie	bed	
3.	soup	tin	
4.	tack	pig	
5.	toy	cup	
6.	tape	log	
7.	fan	toe	
8.	lamp	tub	
9.	time	rose	
10.	corn	top	
		Total:	

_____   _____

Student's Name   Date

#BKCD-407 Webber® Hear It! Say It! Learn It!™ • ©2008 Super Duper® Publications • www.superduperinc.com • 1-800-277-8737

T t

1.			6.		
2.			7.		
3.			8.		
4.			9.		
5.			10.		

#BKCD-407 Webber® Hear It! Say It! Learn It!™ • ©2008 Super Duper® Publications • www.superduperinc.com • 1-800-277-8737

Name _____   Date _____

Learning to Write the Letter Tt

Directions: Introduce the letter **Tt**. Have the student(s) cut out the Letter Flashcard from page 64 and glue or tape the backs of the two flashcards (Picture Symbol and Letter) together. Now, student(s) can refer to **both** sides of the flashcard for reinforcement during the remainder of the chapter.

Say: *This is the letter **Tt**. This (point) is the uppercase **T**. This is the lowercase **t**. The letter **Tt** makes the **Time Sound** /t/. What is the Time Sound?*

Have the student(s) practice forming uppercase **T** and lowercase **t** using the index finger of his/her dominant hand to trace the letters on the flashcards. Demonstrate the action first.

Say: *To make an uppercase **T**, put your finger at the top of the letter. Make a straight line down, like a stick. Pick up your finger and put it back at the top. Make a short line across the top.*

*To make a lowercase **t**, put your finger at the top of the letter. Make a line straight down, like a stick. Make a short line across the middle.*

Note: You may need to modify letter formation and/or verbal cues to best fit with your school's curriculum. For a quick guide to handwriting cues, refer to *Book 2, Appendix C*.

Give each student a copy of the **Time Sound /t/ Worksheet 4**. Student(s) will practice writing uppercase **T** and lowercase **t** with a pencil. First, have the student(s) trace within the outlines. Then, trace along the dotted lines. Finally, have the student(s) practice writing the letter without a guide.

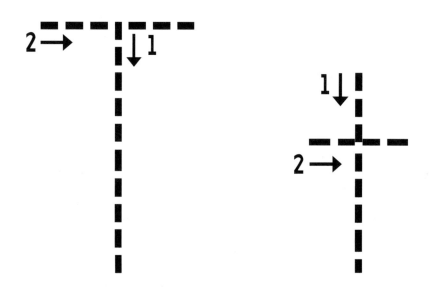

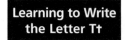

#BKCD-407 Webber® Hear It! Say It! Learn It!™ • ©2008 Super Duper® Publications • www.superduperinc.com • 1-800-277-8737

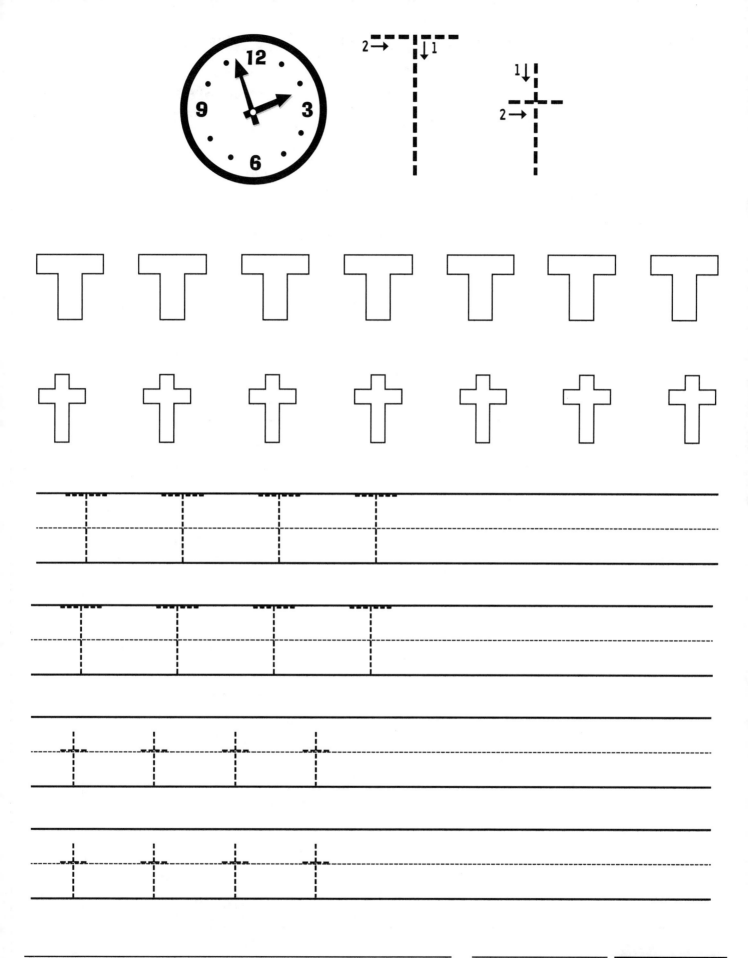

#BKCD-407 Webber® Hear It! Say It! Learn It!™ • ©2008 Super Duper® Publications • www.superduperinc.com • 1-800-277-8737

Time Sound /t/ and Letter Tt in Pictures with Initial Letter

Directions: Give each student a copy of the **Time Sound /t/ Worksheet 5**.

Say: *I'm going to say some words to you. Listen to me say two words each time. If you hear the **Time Sound /t/** at the beginning of the word <u>and</u> see the letter **Tt**, circle the picture and letter that begins with the **Time Sound /t/**. Ready? Number 1, tie - goose, Number 2, tag - king, Number 3, coat - tear, etc.*

To record data for two or more students, see *Book 2, Appendix B*.

 For more practice, choose the **Time Sound /t/** and complete the **Pictures & Letters** activity.

	Word Pair		Check if Correct ✓
1.	Tie	Goose	
2.	tag	king	
3.	coat	tear	
4.	duck	toe	
5.	Time	Pig	
6.	Nail	Tool	
7.	Hen	Tack	
8.	toad	farm	
9.	Tent	Door	
10.	rug	top	
		Total:	

#BKCD-407 Webber® Hear It! Say It! Learn It!™ • ©2008 Super Duper® Publications • www.superduperinc.com • 1-800-277-8737

_____   _____
Student's Name   Date

1.		T			G
2.		t			k
3.		c			t
4.		d			t
5.		T			P
6.		N			T
7.		H			T
8.		t			f
9.		T			D
10.		r			t

_____
Name

_____
Date

Practice Writing the Letter Tt

Directions: Give each student a copy of the **Time Sound /t/ Worksheet 6**.

Say: *I'm going to say some sounds, one at a time. If you hear the **Time Sound /t/**, write an uppercase **T** on the ticket. If you hear a different sound, put an X on the ticket. Ready? Ticket Number 1, /t/, Number 2, /t/, Number 3, /m/, etc.*

Practice writing a lowercase **t** using Trial 2 stimuli on an additional copy of **Worksheet 6**. To record data for two or more students, see *Book 2, Appendix B*.

	Trial 1			Trial 2		
	Stimulus Sound	**Correctly Identified /t/ Sound**	**Correctly Wrote Uppercase T**	**Stimulus Sound**	**Correctly Identified /t/ Sound**	**Correctly Wrote Lowercase t**
1.	/t/			/f/		
2.	/t/			/t/		
3.	/m/			/p/		
4.	/v/			/t/		
5.	/t/			/t/		
6.	/g/			/k/		
7.	/t/			/s/		
8.	/t/			/b/		
9.	/n/			/t/		
10.	/p/			/t/		
	Total:			**Total:**		

_____   _____

Student's Name   Date

**Scoresheet 6
Writing Tt**

#BKCD-407 Webber® Hear It! Say It! Learn It!™ • ©2008 Super Duper® Publications • www.superduperinc.com • 1-800-277-8737

T t

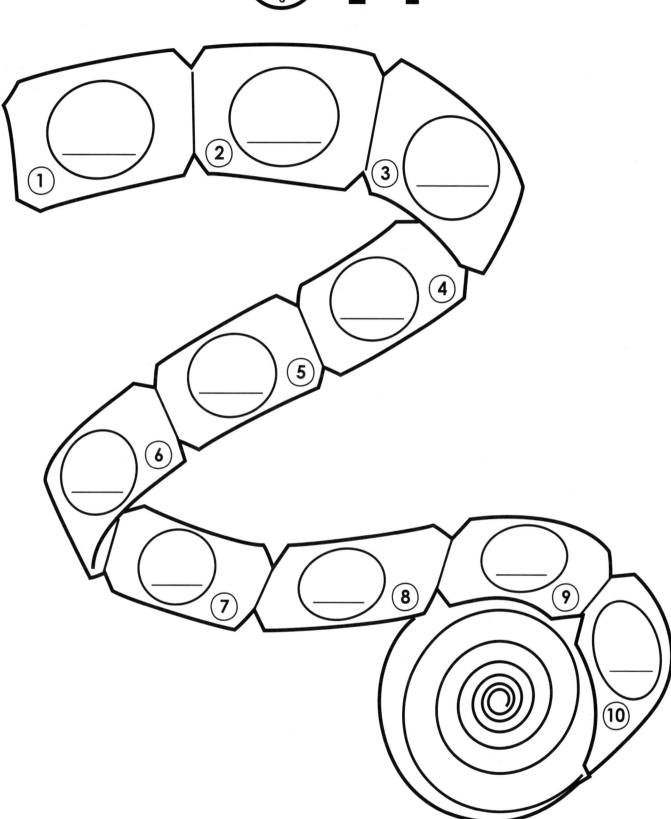

Time Sound /t/ and Letter Tt in Pictures and Words

Directions: Give each student a copy of the **Time Sound /t/ Worksheet 7**.

Say: *On this paper, we see pictures with words beside them. Look at the pictures and words on the first row. Say the word that names each picture. If the word starts with the* **Time Sound /t/** *and you see the letter* **Tt***, put a circle on that picture. Ready? Number 1, toys - boys, Number 2, men - ten, Number 3, tie - pie, etc.*

To record data for two or more students, see *Book 2, Appendix B.*

 For more practice, choose the **Time Sound /t/** and complete the **Pictures & Words** activity.

	Word Pair		Check if Correct ✓
1.	toy	boy	
2.	men	ten	
3.	Tie	Pie	
4.	Tack	Back	
5.	sail	tail	
6.	dime	time	
7.	Toe	Hoe	
8.	mop	top	
9.	Tag	Wag	
10.	Fire	Tire	
		Total:	

_____   _____
Student's Name   Date

#BKCD-407 Webber® Hear It! Say It! Learn It!™ • ©2008 Super Duper® Publications • www.superduperinc.com • 1-800-277-8737

 **T t**

1.		toy			boy
2.		men	**10**		ten
3.		Tie			Pie
4.		Tack			Back
5.		sail			tail
6.		dime			time
7.		Toe			Hoe
8.		mop			top
9.		Tag			Wag
10.		Fire			Tire

Name   Date

#BKCD-407 Webber® Hear It! Say It! Learn It!™ • ©2008 Super Duper® Publications • www.superduperinc.com • 1-800-277-8737

Time Sound /t/ and the Letter Tt in Words

Directions: Give each student a copy of the **Time Sound /t/ Worksheet 8**.

Say: *On this paper, we see a list of words. Some of them begin with the letter **Tt** which makes the **Time Sound /t/**. I'm going to say two words each time. Point to each word as I say it. Circle the word that begins with the letter **Tt** and the **Time Sound /t/**. Ready? Number 1, ten - pen, Number 2, tub - rub, Number 3, tell - bell, etc.*

To record data for two or more students, see *Book 2, Appendix B*.

 For more practice, choose the **Time Sound /t/** and complete the **Words** activity.

	Word Pair		Check if Correct ✓
1.	Ten	Pen	
2.	tub	rub	
3.	tell	bell	
4.	pie	tie	
5.	kick	tick	
6.	Tag	Lag	
7.	same	tame	
8.	Toad	Road	
9.	duck	tuck	
10.	ton	son	
		Total:	

_____   _____
Student's Name   Date

Scoresheet 8 /t/ in Words

#BKCD-407 Webber® Hear It! Say It! Learn It!™ • ©2008 Super Duper® Publications • www.superduperinc.com • 1-800-277-8737

1.	Ten	Pen
2.	tub	rub
3.	tell	bell
4.	pie	tie
5.	kick	tick
6.	Tag	Lag
7.	same	tame
8.	Toad	Road
9.	duck	tuck
10.	ton	son

_____   _____
Name   Date

Extension Activity for the Time Sound /t/

Use a large clock that has hands you can easily manipulate, or draw a large clock face on the chalkboard. Together as a group, count the hours of the clock: "One o'clock, two o'clock, three o'clock...etc." Ask the students to help find two o'clock, ten o'clock, and twelve o'clock. Teach the students where to put the hands of the clock for each time.

After completing the activity, gather the class around a story chart or chalkboard. Ask the students to tell you about the activity. Write their comments on the chart/board. Then, read the sentences together. You should not expect the students to be able to read the story, but they will begin to connect fluent speech with written text and recognize words beginning with the target sound.

Lead the students through a retelling of the activity in the following manner:

1. If possible, use a tape recorder to record the students' sentences about the activity.

2. Replay the taped sentences and write them on the board.

3. After writing each sentence, read each sentence once.

4. Have the class "read" the sentences a second time along with you.

5. As the students read the sentences aloud, move a pointer (or your finger) in a continuous, fluid motion across the words.

6. Encourage the students to come up one by one and point to any words that begin with the target sound and letter (**Time Sound /t/**).

See example sentences for this activity below.

"We can **tell time**."

"I **turned** the big hand **to** the **twelve**."

"Joey **turned** the **tiny** hand **to** the **ten**."

"The **time** says **two** o'clock."

Create your own activity and story using the **Time Sound /t/**!

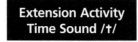

Extension Activity
Time Sound /t/

#BKCD-407 Webber® Hear It! Say It! Learn It!™ • ©2008 Super Duper® Publications • www.superduperinc.com • 1-800-277-8737

Unit 2

Baby Sound /g/ → Gg
Pages 85–104

Popcorn Sound /p/ → Pp
Pages 105–124

Drum Sound /d/ → Dd
Pages 125–144

Rooster Sound /k/ → Kk/Cc
Pages 145–168

Baby Sound /g/
Introducing the Baby Sound /g/

Introduce the **Baby Sound /g/** by reading the script below to the student(s). Demonstrate and discuss the formation of the **Baby Sound /g/** (see *Resource Book 2*, Appendix A for a description of the **Baby Sound /g/**).

Say: *Today we are going to learn about the **Baby Sound /g/**. Watch me say the **Baby Sound**: /g/ (pause) /g/ (pause) /g/. Now it's your turn to make the **Baby Sound /g/**.*

Have the students practice the **Baby Sound /g/** aloud. Then, ask the questions in the table below.

Lips	What are your lips doing when you say the **Baby Sound /g/**?
Tongue	Do you use your tongue to say the **Baby Sound /g/**?
Breath	Is there a burst of air or a long flow of air when you say the **Baby Sound /g/**?
Voice	Feel your neck when you say the **Baby Sound /g/**. Can you feel any vibration? This is called voice. The **Baby Sound /g/** has voice.

Have the student(s) cut out the Picture Symbol Flashcard on page 86. Student(s) can refer to this picture symbol for reinforcement during the Auditory Bombardment Story and throughout the first part of the chapter (Worksheets 1–3).

Note: You will be prompted to create the Letter Flashcard with Worksheet 4.

# G g

Picture Symbol Flashcard

Letter Flashcard

/g/ Flashcards

#BKCD-407 Webber® Hear It! Say It! Learn It!™ • ©2008 Super Duper® Publications • www.superduperinc.com • 1-800-277-8737

Baby Sound /g/
Auditory Bombardment Story

Directions: Read the story aloud to the student(s) or play it from the CD-ROM.

 Note: You have the option of having "No Text" (for auditory bombardment) or "Text" (for letter/word recognition and reading).

Giggly Garret Gomez

Garret Gomez was a giggly baby who was always getting into things. One day, Garret's grandma, Gail, found Garret just as he began to give his dog one of her gold earrings. Garret giggled in delight, "*g, g, g!*" Grandpa Gunther decided to give Gail a break for a while. "Let's go to the grocery store, Garret," Grandpa suggested. Grandma Gail warned, "Garret is a handful in the grocery store. Keep your eye on him, Gunther!" Garret giggled in agreement, "*g, g, g.*"

At the grocery store, Garret tried to grab a can of green beans as Grandpa Gunther pushed the grocery cart. Garret's little hand knocked one can into another and before Grandpa Gunther could stop them, dozens of cans of green beans went crashing to the ground. While Grandpa Gunther gathered the cans of green beans, Garret giggled, "*g, g, g.*" Grandpa Gunther decided to watch Garret more closely and moved along to get the rest of the groceries—eggs, bagels, grapes, hot dogs, and sugar.

In the checkout line, the grocery store clerk put all of the food in a big, brown bag with the eggs on top, so they would not get crushed. But as Grandpa Gunther gave the clerk money for the groceries, Garret tried to grab the eggs. His tiny little hand tipped over the big, brown bag and all of the groceries spilled out. The eggs broke, and the gooey yokes soaked everything. All of the groceries became soggy. Garret giggled with glee, "*g, g, g!*" Grandpa Gunther shrugged and patted Garret's head, "I guess the next time we go to the grocery store, we'll bring Grandma Gail to help us."

/g/ Auditory
Bombardment

Baby Sound /g/ in Isolation

Directions: Give each student a copy of the **Baby Sound /g/ Worksheet 1**.

Say: *I'm going to say some sounds, one at a time. If you hear the **Baby Sound /g/**, put a check mark (✓) on the goose. If you hear a different sound, put an X on the goose. Ready? Number 1, /g/, Number 2, /g/, Number 3, /t/, etc.*

Use additional blank copies of **Worksheet 1** for the sound stimuli in Trial 2 and Trial 3 below. To record data for two or more students, see *Book 2, Appendix B*.

 For more practice, choose the **Baby Sound /g/** and complete the **Isolation** activity.

	Trial 1		Trial 2		Trial 3	
	Stimulus Sound	**Check if Correct** ✓	**Stimulus Sound**	**Check if Correct** ✓	**Stimulus Sound**	**Check if Correct** ✓
1.	/g/		/g/		/g/	
2.	/g/		/b/		/n/	
3.	/t/		/f/		/g/	
4.	/l/		/g/		/b/	
5.	/g/		/g/		/f/	
6.	/n/		/n/		/g/	
7.	/f/		/l/		/b/	
8.	/g/		/g/		/l/	
9.	/m/		/f/		/g/	
10.	/g/		/g/		/g/	
	Total:		Total:		Total:	

_____   _____   **Scoresheet 1 /g/ in Isolation**
Student's Name   Date

#BKCD-407 Webber® Hear It! Say It! Learn It!™ • ©2008 Super Duper® Publications • www.superduperinc.com • 1-800-277-8737

G g

Trial _____

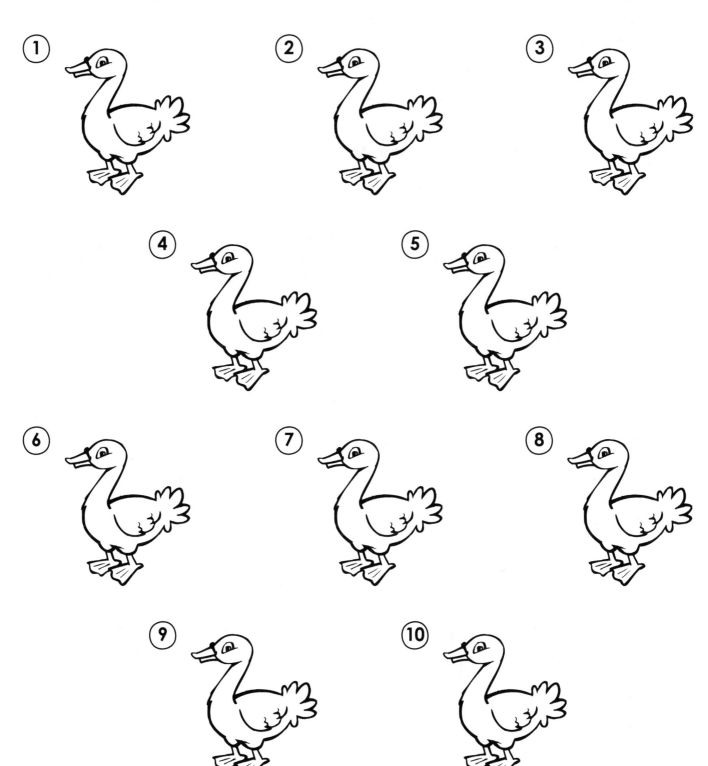

1   2   3

4   5

6   7   8

9   10

_____   _____
Name   Date

Worksheet 1
/g/ in Isolation

Baby Sound /g/ in Syllables

Directions: Give each student a copy of the **Baby Sound /g/ Worksheet 2**.

Say: *I'm going to say some silly words to you, one at a time. If you hear the **Baby Sound /g/** in the silly word, circle the ghost. If you hear a different sound, put an X on the ghost. Ready? Number 1, go-go, Number 2, no-no, Number 3, go-go, etc.*

Use additional blank copies of **Worksheet 2** for the sound stimuli in Trial 2 and Trial 3 below. To record data for two or more students, see *Book 2, Appendix B*.

 For more practice, choose the **Baby Sound /g/** and complete the **Syllables** activity.

	Trial 1		Trial 2		Trial 3	
	Stimulus Sound	**Check if Correct** ✓	**Stimulus Sound**	**Check if Correct** ✓	**Stimulus Sound**	**Check if Correct** ✓
1.	go-go		lo-lo		goo-goo	
2.	no-no		ga-ga		la-la	
3.	go-go		go-go		gee-gee	
4.	so-so		fa-fa		ga-ga	
5.	bo-bo		go-go		do-do	
6.	go-go		wa-wa		go-go	
7.	go-go		sa-sa		pa-pa	
8.	do-do		do-do		fee-fee	
9.	go-go		ga-ga		goo-goo	
10.	fo-fo		go-go		go-go	
	Total:		**Total:**		**Total:**	

_____ _____ **Scoresheet 2 /g/ in Syllables**
Student's Name   Date

#BKCD-407 Webber® Hear It! Say It! Learn It!™ • ©2008 Super Duper® Publications • www.superduperinc.com • 1-800-277-8737

 # G g

 ①  ②  ③

 ④  ⑤

 ⑥  ⑦  ⑧

 ⑨  ⑩

_____ _____
Name   Date

Worksheet 2
/g/ in Syllables

Baby Sound /g/ in Pictures

Directions: Give each student a copy of the **Baby Sound /g/ Worksheet 3**.

Say: *I'm going to say some words to you. Listen to me say two words each time. If you hear the **Baby Sound /g/** at the beginning of the word, circle the picture that begins with the **Baby Sound /g/**. Ready? Number 1, game - robe, Number 2, head - gate, Number 3, nail - gift, etc.*

To record data for two or more students, see *Book 2, Appendix B*.

 For more practice, choose the **Baby Sound /g/** and complete the **Pictures** activity.

	Word Pair		Check if Correct ✓
1.	**g**ame	robe	
2.	head	**g**ate	
3.	nail	**g**ift	
4.	**g**oat	cake	
5.	**g**olf	rat	
6.	milk	**g**own	
7.	**g**um	foot	
8.	bike	**g**irl	
9.	**g**eese	jump	
10.	paw	**g**as	
		Total:	

_____   _____
Student's Name   Date

G g

Learning to Write the Letter Gg

Directions: Introduce the letter **Gg**. Have the student(s) cut out the Letter Flashcard from page 86 and glue or tape the backs of the two flashcards (Picture Symbol and Letter) together. Now, student(s) can refer to **both** sides of the flashcard for reinforcement during the remainder of the chapter.

Say: *This is the letter **Gg**. This (point) is the uppercase **G**. This is the lowercase **g**. The letter **Gg** makes the **Baby Sound /g/**. What is the Baby Sound?*

Have the student(s) practice forming uppercase **G** and lowercase **g** using the index finger of his/her dominant hand to trace the letters on the flashcards. Demonstrate the action first.

Say: *To make an uppercase **G**, put your finger at the top of the letter. Make part of a bubble. Make a short line inside of the bubble, and a short line down to the bottom.*

*To make a lowercase **g** put your finger at the top of the letter. Make a small bubble. Attach a hook to the bubble.*

Note: You may need to modify letter formation and/or verbal cues to best fit with your school's curriculum. For a quick guide to handwriting cues, refer to *Book 2, Appendix C*.

Give each student a copy of the **Baby Sound /g/ Worksheet 4**. Student(s) will practice writing uppercase **G** and lowercase **g** with a pencil. First, have the student(s) trace within the outlines. Then, trace along the dotted lines. Finally, have the student(s) practice writing the letter without a guide.

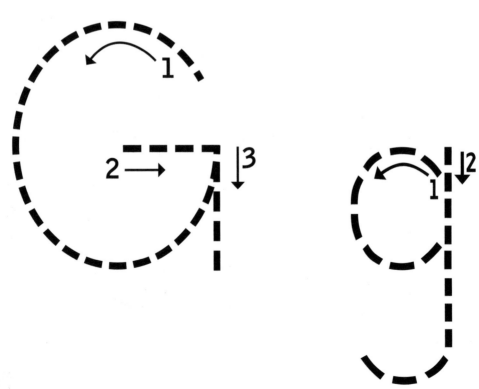

Learning to Write the Letter Gg

#BKCD-407 Webber® Hear It! Say It! Learn It!™ • ©2008 Super Duper® Publications • www.superduperinc.com • 1-800-277-8737

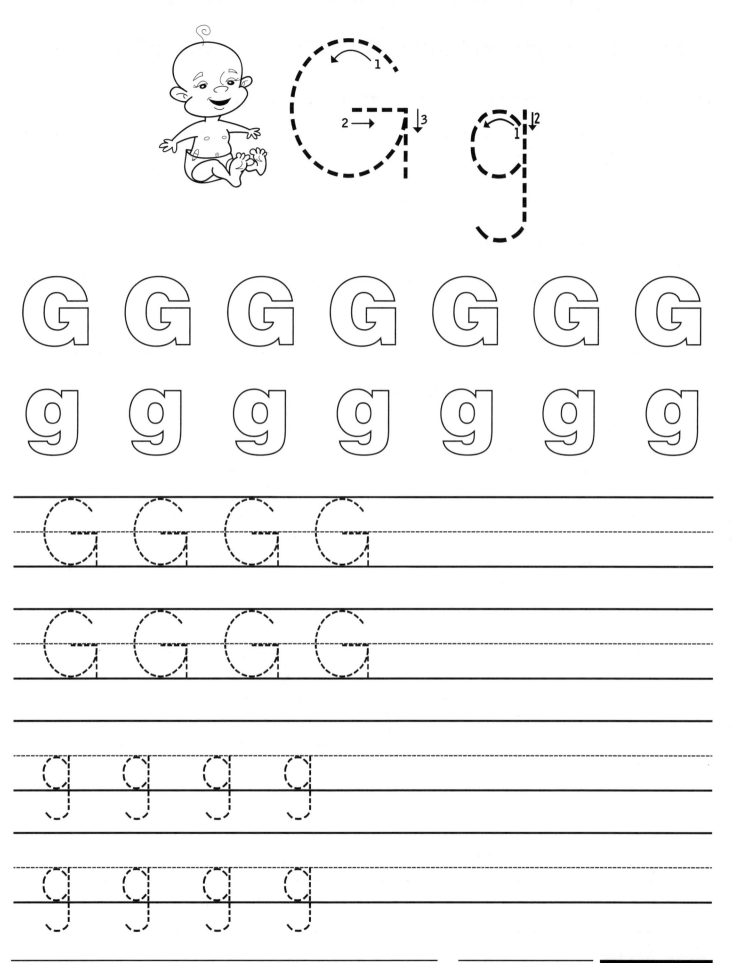

Name _____   Date _____

Worksheet 4
Writing Gg

Baby Sound /g/ and Letter Gg in Pictures with Initial Letter

Directions: Give each student a copy of the **Baby Sound /g/ Worksheet 5**.

Say: *I'm going to say some words. Listen to me say two words each time. If you hear the* **Baby Sound /g/** *at the beginning of the word* <u>and</u> *see the letter* **Gg***, circle the picture and letter that begins with the* **Baby Sound /g/***. Ready? Number 1, goat - bed, Number 2, bike - gate, Number 3, girl - jump, etc.*

To record data for two or more students, see *Book 2, Appendix B.*

 For more practice, choose the **Baby Sound /g/** and complete the **Pictures & Letters** activity.

	Word Pair		Check if Correct ✓
1.	**G**oat	Bed	
2.	bike	**g**ate	
3.	**g**irl	jump	
4.	Moon	**G**olf	
5.	**g**as	cake	
6.	pail	**g**ift	
7.	**G**own	Fan	
8.	Duck	**G**um	
9.	Hat	**G**host	
10.	**g**ame	tail	
		Total:	

_____   _____
Student's Name   Date

#BKCD-407 Webber® Hear It! Say It! Learn It!™ • ©2008 Super Duper® Publications • www.superduperinc.com • 1-800-277-8737

 # G g

1.		G			B
2.		b			g
3.		g			j
4.		M			G
5.		g			c
6.		p			g
7.		G			F
8.		D			G
9.		H			G
10.		g			t

_____   _____

Name   Date

#BKCD-407 Webber® Hear It! Say It! Learn It!™ • ©2008 Super Duper® Publications • www.superduperinc.com • 1-800-277-8737

Practice Writing the Letter Gg

Directions: Give each student a copy of the **Baby Sound /g/ Worksheet 6**.

Say: *I'm going to say some sounds, one at a time. If you hear the **Baby Sound /g/**, write an uppercase **G** on the goat. If you hear a different sound, put an X on the goat. Ready? Goat Number 1, /g/, Number 2, /m/, Number 3, /f/, etc.*

Practice writing a lowercase **g** using Trial 2 stimuli on an additional copy of **Worksheet 6**. To record data for two or more students, see *Book 2, Appendix B*.

	Trial 1			Trial 2		
	Stimulus Sound	Correctly Identified /g/ Sound	Correctly Wrote Uppercase G	Stimulus Sound	Correctly Identified /g/ Sound	Correctly Wrote Lowercase g
1.	/g/			/g/		
2.	/m/			/t/		
3.	/f/			/g/		
4.	/g/			/d/		
5.	/g/			/b/		
6.	/p/			/g/		
7.	/b/			/g/		
8.	/g/			/k/		
9.	/n/			/g/		
10.	/g/			/v/		
	Total:			Total:		

_____   _____

Student's Name   Date

Scoresheet 6
Writing Gg

#BKCD-407 Webber® Hear It! Say It! Learn It!™ • ©2008 Super Duper® Publications • www.superduperinc.com • 1-800-277-8737

G g

Trial _____

_____
Name

_____
Date

**Worksheet 6
Writing Gg**

Baby Sound /g/ and Letter Gg in Pictures and Words

Directions: Give each student a copy of the **Baby Sound /g/ Worksheet 7**.

Say: *On this paper, we see pictures with words beside them. Look at the pictures and words on the first row. Say the word that names each picture. If the word starts with the **Baby Sound /g/** <u>and</u> you see the letter **Gg**, put a circle on that picture. Ready? Number 1, goose - moose, Number 2, date - gate, Number 3, gill - pill, etc.*

To record data for two or more students, see *Book 2, Appendix B*.

 For more practice, choose the **Baby Sound /g/** and complete the **Pictures & Words** activity.

	Word Pair		Check if Correct ✓
1.	**g**oose	moose	
2.	Date	**G**ate	
3.	**G**ill	Pill	
4.	Hum	**G**um	
5.	**g**ood	wood	
6.	**g**ear	tear	
7.	old	**g**old	
8.	**G**oat	Coat	
9.	fame	**g**ame	
10.	**G**uy	Buy	
		Total:	

_____   _____
Student's Name   Date

Scoresheet 7 /g/ Pictures and Words

#BKCD-407 Webber® Hear It! Say It! Learn It!™ • ©2008 Super Duper® Publications • www.superduperinc.com • 1-800-277-8737

 # G g

1.		**g**oose		moose
2.		Date		**G**ate
3.		**G**ill		Pill
4.		Hum		**G**um
5.		**g**ood		wood
6.		**g**ear		tear
7.		old		**g**old
8.		**G**oat		Coat
9.		fame		**g**ame
10.		**G**uy		Buy

_____   _____
Name   Date

Worksheet 7
/g/ in Pictures
and Words

#BKCD-407 Webber® Hear It! Say It! Learn It!™ • ©2008 Super Duper® Publications • www.superduperinc.com • 1-800-277-8737

Baby Sound /g/ and the Letter Gg in Words

Directions: Give each student a copy of the **Baby Sound /g/ Worksheet 8**.

Say: *On this paper, we see a list of words. Some of them begin with the letter* **Gg** *which makes the* **Baby Sound /g/.** *I'm going to say two words each time. Point to each word as I say it. Circle the word that begins with the letter* **Gg** *and the* **Baby Sound /g/.** *Ready? Number 1, go - no, Number 2, get - set, Number 3, coal - goal, etc.*

To record data for two or more students, see *Book 2, Appendix B.*

 For more practice, choose the **Baby Sound /g/** and complete the **Words** activity.

	Word Pair		Check if Correct ✓
1.	**g**o	no	
2.	**g**et	set	
3.	Coal	**G**oal	
4.	Bill	**G**ill	
5.	**G**ust	Dust	
6.	boat	**g**oat	
7.	**g**oose	loose	
8.	Rain	**G**ain	
9.	live	**g**ive	
10.	**g**ate	late	
		Total:	

_____   _____

Scoresheet 8 /g/ in Words

#BKCD-407 Webber® Hear It! Say It! Learn It!™ • ©2008 Super Duper® Publications • www.superduperinc.com • 1-800-277-8737

 # G g

1.	go	no
2.	get	set
3.	Coal	Goal
4.	Bill	Gill
5.	Gust	Dust
6.	boat	goat
7.	goose	loose
8.	Rain	Gain
9.	live	give
10.	gate	late

_____ _____

Name   Date

#BKCD-407 Webber® Hear It! Say It! Learn It!™ • ©2008 Super Duper® Publications • www.superduperinc.com • 1-800-277-8737

Extension Activity for the Baby Sound /g/

Have the student(s) help you plan a pretend trip to the grocery store. Brainstorm with the students all of the items you might see in a grocery store that begin with the **Baby Sound /g/**, such as green beans and grapes.

After completing the activity, gather the class around a story chart or chalkboard. Ask the students to tell you about the activity. Write their comments on the chart/board. Then, read the sentences together. You should not expect the students to be able to read the story, but they will begin to connect fluent speech with written text and recognize words beginning with the target sound.

Lead the students through a retelling of the activity in the following manner:

1. If possible, use a tape recorder to record the students' sentences about the activity.

2. Replay the taped sentences and write them on the board.

3. After writing each sentence, read each sentence once.

4. Have the class "read" the sentences a second time along with you.

5. As the students read the sentences aloud, move a pointer (or your finger) in a continuous, fluid motion across the words.

6. Encourage the students to come up one by one and point to any words that begin with the target sound and letter (**Baby Sound /g/**).

See example sentences for this activity below.

"We are **going** to the **grocery** store."

"We are **going** to **get green** beans."

"We are **going** to **get grapes**."

"We are **going** to **get grits**."

Create your own activity and story using the **Baby Sound /g/**!

#BKCD-407 Webber® Hear It! Say It! Learn It!™ • ©2008 Super Duper® Publications • www.superduperinc.com • 1-800-277-8737

Popcorn Sound /p/
Introducing the Popcorn Sound /p/

Introduce the **Popcorn Sound /p/** by reading the script below to the student(s). Demonstrate and discuss the formation of the **Popcorn Sound /p/** (see *Resource Book 2*, Appendix A for a description of the **Popcorn Sound /p/**).

Say: *Today we are going to learn about the* **Popcorn Sound /p/**. *Watch me say the* **Popcorn Sound**: **/p/** *(pause)* **/p/** *(pause)* **/p/**. *Now it's your turn to make the* **Popcorn Sound /p/**.

Have the student(s) practice the **Popcorn Sound /p/** aloud. Then, ask the questions in the table below.

Lips	*What are your lips doing when you say the* **Popcorn Sound /p/**?
Tongue	*Do you use your tongue to say the* **Popcorn Sound /p/**?
Breath	*Is there a burst of air or a long flow of air when you say the* **Popcorn Sound /p/**?
Voice	*Feel your neck when you say the* **Popcorn Sound /p/**. *Can you feel any vibration? That is because the* **Popcorn Sound /p/** *does not have voice.*

Have the student(s) cut out the Picture Symbol Flashcard on page 106. Student(s) can refer to this picture symbol for reinforcement during the Auditory Bombardment Story and throughout the first part of the chapter (Worksheets 1–3).

Note: You will be prompted to create the Letter Flashcard with Worksheet 4.

 # P p

Picture Symbol Flashcard

Letter Flashcard

/p/ Flashcards

#BKCD-407 Webber® Hear It! Say It! Learn It!™ • ©2008 Super Duper® Publications • www.superduperinc.com • 1-800-277-8737

Popcorn Sound /p/
Auditory Bombardment Story

Directions: Read the story aloud to the student(s) or play it from the CD-ROM.

 Note: You have the option of having "No Text" (for auditory bombardment) or "Text" (for letter/word recognition and reading).

Princess Pajama Party

Pamela **P**atterson was **p**lanning a **p**ajama **p**arty with a **p**rincess theme. Her dad, **P**aul, took her to the **p**arty shop to **p**urchase her **p**arty supplies. **P**amela **p**icked out **p**rincess **p**lates, napkins, and cups. She was **p**ositive everything would be **p**erfect!

The night of the **p**arty, **P**amela's friends **p**iled into the house already wearing their **p**ajamas. Some girls were in **p**ink, some in **p**urple, and one girl even wore **p**olka dot **p**ajamas.

While **P**amela and her **p**als were in the **p**layroom **p**retending to be **p**retty **p**rincesses, they heard a strange **p**opping sound—***p, p, p.*** "What was that ***p, p, p*** sound I just heard," asked the **p**rincess in **p**olka dots. **P**amela shrugged, "It's **p**ossibly a **p**uppy **p**rancing around upstairs, or maybe the **p**eanuts are spilling in the **p**antry." They heard the sound again—***p, p, p.*** They stopped **p**laying and tip-toed upstairs.

When they **p**eered into the kitchen, they saw **P**aul holding a **p**an on the stovetop. The **p**opping sound was fast and loud—***p, p, p.*** The **p**retty **p**rincesses **p**aused a minute, trying to be **p**atient. They watched as **P**aul **p**icked up the lid on the **p**an. Everyone was **p**leased to see it **p**iled full of **p**opcorn. **P**amela and her **p**retty **p**rincess **p**als ate the **p**opcorn and **p**layed until it was time to sleep. Before **P**amela **p**ut her head on her **p**illow that night, she said, "Thanks, Dad, for a **p**erfect **p**rincess **p**ajama **p**arty."

Popcorn Sound /p/ in Isolation

Directions: Give each student a copy of the **Popcorn Sound /p/ Worksheet 1**.

Say: *I'm going to say some sounds, one at a time. If you hear the **Popcorn Sound /p/**, put a check mark (✓) on the peanut. If you hear a different sound, put an X on the peanut. Ready? Number 1, /p/, Number 2, /p/, Number 3, /m/, etc.*

Use additional blank copies of **Worksheet 1** for the sound stimuli in Trial 2 and Trial 3 below. To record data for two or more students, see *Book 2, Appendix B*.

 For more practice, choose the **Popcorn Sound /p/** and complete the **Isolation** activity.

	Trial 1		Trial 2		Trial 3	
	Stimulus Sound	Check if Correct ✓	Stimulus Sound	Check if Correct ✓	Stimulus Sound	Check if Correct ✓
1.	/p/		/b/		/p/	
2.	/p/		/n/		/s/	
3.	/m/		/p/		/f/	
4.	/d/		/k/		/p/	
5.	/p/		/v/		/p/	
6.	/p/		/p/		/k/	
7.	/s/		/p/		/m/	
8.	/t/		/g/		/p/	
9.	/p/		/p/		/t/	
10.	/g/		/m/		/p/	
	Total:		Total:		Total:	

_____   _____   **Scoresheet 1 /p/ in Isolation**

108   #BKCD-407 Webber® Hear It! Say It! Learn It!™ • ©2008 Super Duper® Publications • www.superduperinc.com • 1-800-277-8737

 **P p**

 ①

 ②

 ③

 ④

 ⑤

 ⑥

 ⑦

 ⑧

 ⑨

 ⑩

_____   _____
Name   Date

Worksheet 1
/p/ in Isolation

Popcorn Sound /p/ in Syllables

Directions: Give each student a copy of the **Popcorn Sound /p/ Worksheet 2**.

Say: *I'm going to say some silly words to you, one at a time. If you hear the **Popcorn Sound /p/** in the silly word, circle the pig. If you hear a different sound, put an X on the pig. Ready? Number 1, po-po, Number 2, to-to, Number 3, po-po, etc.*

Use additional blank copies of **Worksheet 2** for the sound stimuli in Trial 2 and Trial 3 below. To record data for two or more students, see *Book 2, Appendix B*.

 For more practice, choose the **Popcorn Sound /p/** and complete the **Syllables** activity.

	Trial 1		Trial 2		Trial 3	
	Stimulus Sound	**Check if Correct** ✓	**Stimulus Sound**	**Check if Correct** ✓	**Stimulus Sound**	**Check if Correct** ✓
1.	po-po		pa-pa		puh-puh	
2.	to-to		vo-vo		po-po	
3.	po-po		ga-ga		dee-dee	
4.	po-po		po-po		pa-pa	
5.	do-do		lo-lo		loo-loo	
6.	so-so		na-na		ko-ko	
7.	po-po		po-po		pay-pay	
8.	fo-fo		pa-pa		soo-soo	
9.	mo-mo		ra-ra		po-po	
10.	po-po		so-so		muh-muh	
	Total:		**Total:**		**Total:**	

_____   _____

Student's Name   Date

#BKCD-407 Webber® Hear It! Say It! Learn It!™ • ©2008 Super Duper® Publications • www.superduperinc.com • 1-800-277-8737

 **P p**

①

②

③

④

⑤

⑥

⑦

⑧

⑨

⑩

_____   _____
Name   Date

Worksheet 2
/p/ in Syllables

Popcorn Sound /p/ in Pictures

Directions: Give each student a copy of the **Popcorn Sound /p/ Worksheet 3**.

Say: *I'm going to say some words to you. Listen to me say two words each time. If you hear the **Popcorn Sound /p/** at the beginning of the word, circle the picture that begins with the **Popcorn Sound /p/**. Ready? Number 1, pan - hat, Number 2, jam - paw, Number 3, rat - pear, etc.*

To record data for two or more students, see *Book 2, Appendix B*.

 For more practice, choose the **Popcorn Sound /p/** and complete the **Pictures** activity.

	Word Pair		Check if Correct ✓
1.	**p**an	hat	
2.	jam	**p**aw	
3.	rat	**p**ear	
4.	**p**en	seal	
5.	**p**ie	hut	
6.	dog	**p**ole	
7.	lamp	**p**ig	
8.	**p**ool	seed	
9.	bell	**p**ea	
10.	jet	**p**ot	
		Total:	

_____   _____

Scoresheet 3 /p/ in Pictures

#BKCD-407 Webber® Hear It! Say It! Learn It!™ • ©2008 Super Duper® Publications • www.superduperinc.com • 1-800-277-8737

P p

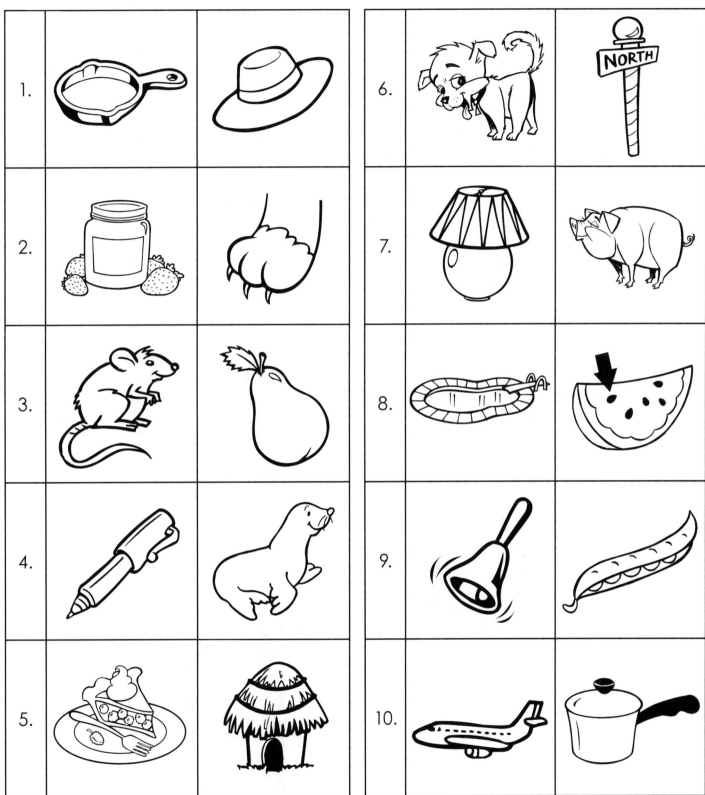

#BKCD-407 Webber® Hear It! Say It! Learn It!™ • ©2008 Super Duper® Publications • www.superduperinc.com • 1-800-277-8737

Learning to Write the Letter Pp

Directions: Introduce the letter **Pp**. Have the student(s) cut out the Letter Flashcard from page 106 and glue or tape the backs of the two flashcards (Picture Symbol and Letter) together. Now, student(s) can refer to **both** sides of the flashcard for reinforcement during the remainder of the chapter.

Say: *This is the letter **Pp**. This (point) is the uppercase **P**. This is the lowercase **p**. The letter **Pp** makes the **Popcorn Sound /p/**. What is the Popcorn Sound?*

Have the student(s) practice forming uppercase **P** and lowercase **p** using the index finger of his/her dominant hand to trace the letters on their flashcards. Demonstrate the action first.

Say: *To make an uppercase **P**, put your finger at the top of the letter. Make a straight line down, like a stick. Make a small bubble attached to the top of the stick.*

*To make a lowercase **p**, put your finger at the top of the letter. Make a straight line down, like a stick. Make a small bubble attached to the top of the stick.*

Note: You may need to modify letter formation and/or verbal cues to best fit with your school's curriculum. For a quick guide to handwriting cues, refer to *Book 2*, Appendix C.

Give each student a copy of the **Popcorn Sound /p/ Worksheet 4**. Student(s) will practice writing uppercase **P** and lowercase **p** with a pencil. First, have the student(s) trace within the outlines. Then, trace along the dotted lines. Finally, have the student(s) practice writing the letter without a guide.

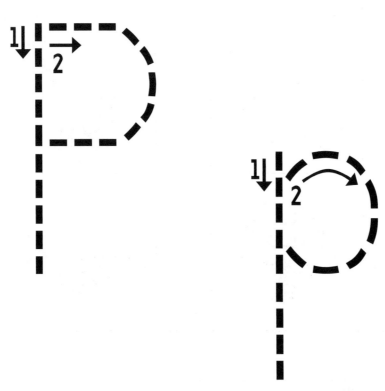

Learning to Write
the Letter Pp

  #BKCD-407 Webber® Hear It! Say It! Learn It!™ • ©2008 Super Duper® Publications • www.superduperinc.com • 1-800-277-8737

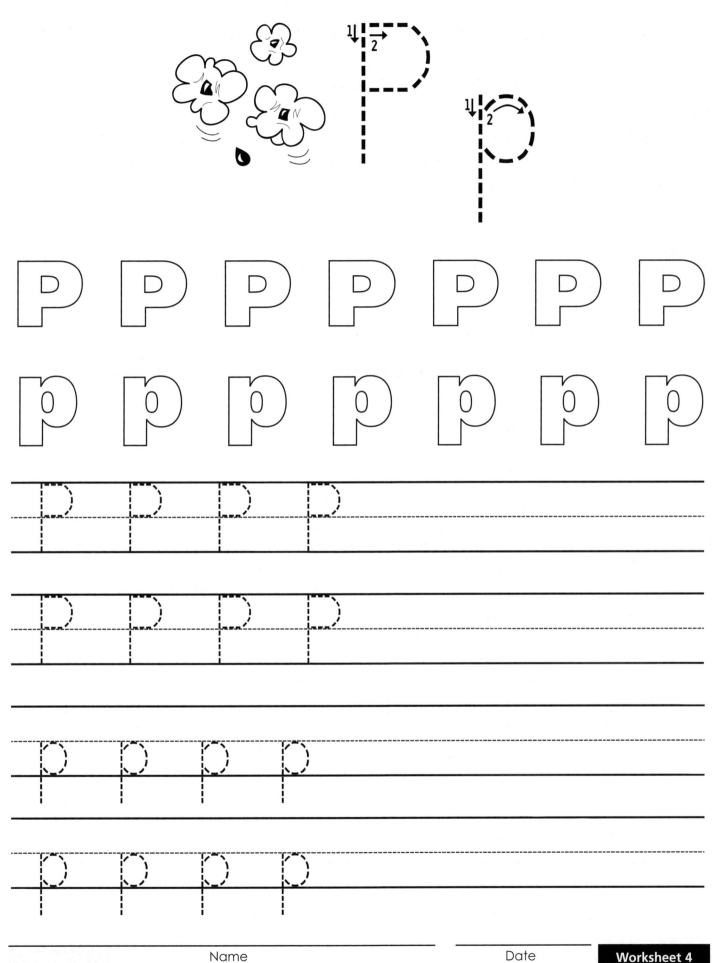

Name

Date

**Worksheet 4
Writing Pp**

Popcorn Sound /p/ and Letter Pp in Pictures with Initial Letter

Directions: Give each student a copy of the **Popcorn Sound /p/ Worksheet 5**.

Say: *I'm going to say some words. Listen to me say two words each time. If you hear the* **Popcorn Sound /p/** *at the beginning of the word <u>and</u> see the letter* **Pp**, *circle the picture and letter that begins with the* **Popcorn Sound /p/**. *Ready? Number 1, pen - dog, Number 2, toe - pig, Number 3, girl - pool, etc.*

To record data for two or more students, see *Book 2, Appendix B*.

 For more practice, choose the **Popcorn Sound /p/** and complete the **Pictures & Letters** activity.

	Word Pair		Check if Correct ✓
1.	**p**en	dog	
2.	toe	**p**ig	
3.	girl	**p**ool	
4.	**P**et	Kick	
5.	Rose	**P**an	
6.	**p**urse	bed	
7.	Farm	**P**ot	
8.	Hen	**P**ear	
9.	**p**ie	moon	
10.	Duck	**P**our	
		Total:	

_____ _____
Student's Name   Date

#BKCD-407 Webber® Hear It! Say It! Learn It!™ • ©2008 Super Duper® Publications • www.superduperinc.com • 1-800-277-8737

Pp

1.		p			d
2.		t			p
3.		g			p
4.		P			K
5.		R			P
6.		p			b
7.		F			P
8.		H			P
9.		p			m
10.		D			P

_____   _____
Name   Date

Worksheet 5
/p/ in Pictures

#BKCD-407 Webber® Hear It! Say It! Learn It!™ • ©2008 Super Duper® Publications • www.superduperinc.com • 1-800-277-8737

Practice Writing the Letter Pp

Directions: Give each student a copy of the **Popcorn Sound /p/ Worksheet 6**.

Say: *I'm going to say some sounds, one at a time. If you hear the **Popcorn Sound /p/**, write an uppercase **P** on the pickle. If you hear a different sound, put an X on the pickle. Ready? Pickle Number 1, /p/, Number 2, /p/, Number 3, /f/, etc.*

Practice writing a lowercase **p** using Trial 2 stimuli on an additional copy of **Worksheet 6**. To record data for two or more students, see *Book 2, Appendix B*.

	Trial 1				Trial 2		
	Stimulus Sound	Correctly Identified /p/ Sound	Correctly Wrote Uppercase P		Stimulus Sound	Correctly Identified /p/ Sound	Correctly Wrote Lowercase p
1.	/p/				/p/		
2.	/p/				/k/		
3.	/f/				/p/		
4.	/g/				/m/		
5.	/p/				/g/		
6.	/k/				/p/		
7.	/p/				/p/		
8.	/p/				/n/		
9.	/d/				/p/		
10.	/p/				/p/		
	Total:				Total:		

_____   _____
Student's Name   Date

Scoresheet 6 Writing Pp

P p

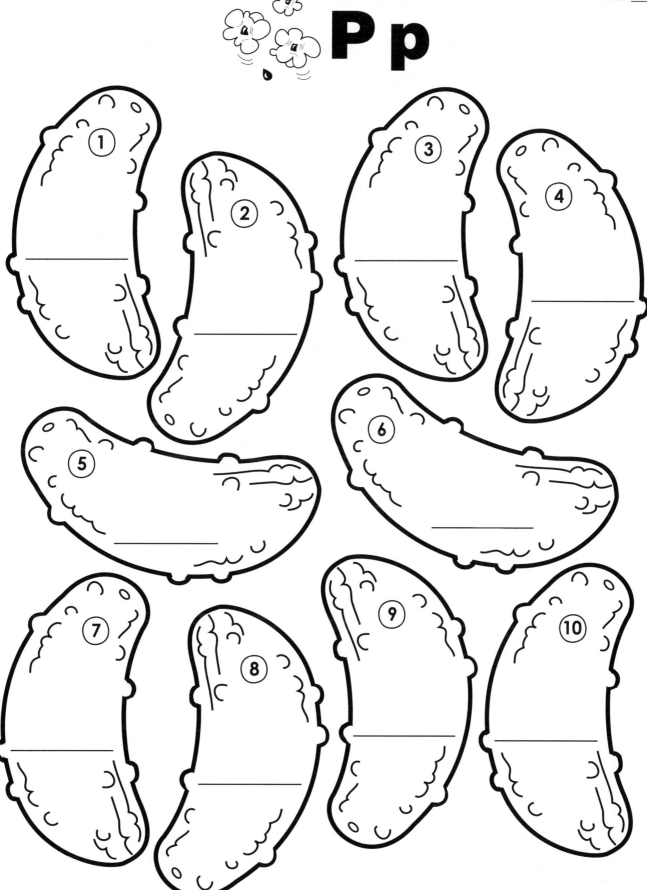

Popcorn Sound /p/ and Letter Pp in Pictures and Words

Directions: Give each student a copy of the **Popcorn Sound /p/ Worksheet 7**.

Say: *On this paper, we see pictures with words beside them. Look at the pictures and words on the first row. Say the word that names each picture. If the word starts with the **Popcorn Sound /p/** <u>and</u> you see the letter **Pp**, put a circle on that picture. Ready? Number 1, pan - fan, Number 2, ten - pen, Number 3, pig - wig, etc.*

To record data for two or more students, see *Book 2, Appendix B.*

 For more practice, choose the **Popcorn Sound /p/** and complete the **Pictures & Words** activity.

	Word Pair		Check if Correct ✓
1.	**P**an	Fan	
2.	ten	**p**en	
3.	**p**ig	wig	
4.	**P**ot	Dot	
5.	**p**ie	tie	
6.	Net	**P**et	
7.	tool	**p**ool	
8.	**p**ull	full	
9.	hat	**p**at	
10.	Tail	**P**ail	
		Total:	

_____   _____
Student's Name   Date

#BKCD-407 Webber® Hear It! Say It! Learn It!™ • ©2008 Super Duper® Publications • www.superduperinc.com • 1-800-277-8737

P p

1.		**P**an		Fan
2.	**10**	ten		**p**en
3.		**p**ig		wig
4.		**P**ot		Dot
5.		**p**ie		tie
6.		Net		**P**et
7.		tool		**p**ool
8.		**p**ull		full
9.		hat		**p**at
10.		Tail		**P**ail

#BKCD-407 Webber® Hear It! Say It! Learn It!™ • ©2008 Super Duper® Publications • www.superduperinc.com • 1-800-277-8737

_____ Name _____ Date

Popcorn Sound /p/ and the Letter Pp in Words

Directions: Give each student a copy of the **Popcorn Sound /p/ Worksheet 8**.

Say: On this paper, we see a list of words. Some of them begin with the letter **Pp** which makes the **Popcorn Sound /p/**. I'm going to say two words each time. Point to each word as I say it. Circle the word that begins with the letter **Pp** and the **Popcorn Sound /p/**. Ready? Number 1, pay - day, Number 2, pat - bat, Number 3, hen - pen, etc.

To record data for two or more students, see *Book 2, Appendix B*.

 For more practice, choose the **Popcorn Sound /p/** and complete the **Words** activity.

	Word Pair		Check if Correct ✓
1.	**P**ay	Day	
2.	**p**at	bat	
3.	hen	**p**en	
4.	Sick	**P**ick	
5.	**p**ine	line	
6.	Get	**P**et	
7.	tin	**p**in	
8.	**P**eel	Feel	
9.	Bear	**P**ear	
10.	**p**ool	cool	
		Total:	

_____   _____
Student's Name   Date

#BKCD-407 Webber® Hear It! Say It! Learn It!™ • ©2008 Super Duper® Publications • www.superduperinc.com • 1-800-277-8737

P p

1.	Pay	Day
2.	pat	bat
3.	hen	pen
4.	Sick	Pick
5.	pine	line
6.	Get	Pet
7.	tin	pin
8.	Peel	Feel
9.	Bear	Pear
10.	pool	cool

_____   _____   **Worksheet 8**
Name   Date   **/p/ in Words**

Extension Activity for the Popcorn Sound /p/

Give watercolors, finger paint, or other type of washable paint to each student. Brainstorm with the student(s) words that begin with the **Popcorn Sound /p/**. Write these words on the chalkboard and read them as a group. Then, have the students paint pictures of objects from this list of words, or any other objects they can think of that start with the **Popcorn Sound /p/**, such as "pig."

After completing the activity, gather the class around a story chart or chalkboard. Ask the students to tell you about the activity. Write their comments on the chart/board. Then, read the sentences together. You should not expect the students to be able to read the story, but they will begin to connect fluent speech with written text and recognize words beginning with the target sound.

Lead the students through a retelling of the activity in the following manner:

1. If possible, use a tape recorder to record the students' sentences about the activity.

2. Replay the taped sentences and write them on the board.

3. After writing each sentence, read each sentence once.

4. Have the class "read" the sentences a second time along with you.

5. As the students read the sentences aloud, move a pointer (or your finger) in a continuous, fluid motion across the words.

6. Encourage the students to come up one by one and point to any words that begin with the target sound and letter (**Popcorn Sound /p/**).

See example sentences for this activity below.

"We **painted pictures**."

"I **painted** a **picture** of a **pig**."

"Becky **painted** a **picture** of a **pot**."

"Mark **painted** a **pool**."

Create your own activity and story using the **Popcorn Sound /p/**!

Extension Activity
Popcorn Sound /p/

Drum Sound /d/
Introducing the Drum Sound /d/

Introduce the **Drum Sound /d/** by reading the script below to the student(s). Demonstrate and discuss the formation of the **Drum Sound /d/** (see *Resource Book 2, Appendix A* for a description of the **Drum Sound /d/**).

Say: *Today we are going to learn about the **Drum Sound /d/**. Watch me say the **Drum Sound**: /d/ (pause) /d/ (pause) /d/. Now it's your turn to make the **Drum Sound /d/**.*

Have the students practice the **Drum Sound /d/** aloud. Then, ask the questions in the table below.

Lips	What are your lips doing when you say the **Drum Sound /d/**?
Tongue	Do you use your tongue to say the **Drum Sound /d/**?
Breath	Is there a burst of air or a long flow of air when you say the **Drum Sound /d/**?
Voice	Feel your neck when you say the **Drum Sound /d/**. Can you feel any vibration? This is called voice. The **Drum Sound /d/** has voice.

Have the student(s) cut out the Picture Symbol Flashcard on page 126. Student(s) can refer to this picture symbol for reinforcement during the Auditory Bombardment Story and throughout the first part of the chapter (Worksheets 1–3).

Note: You will be prompted to create the Letter Flashcard with Worksheet 4.

/d/ Introduction

 **D d**

Picture Symbol Flashcard

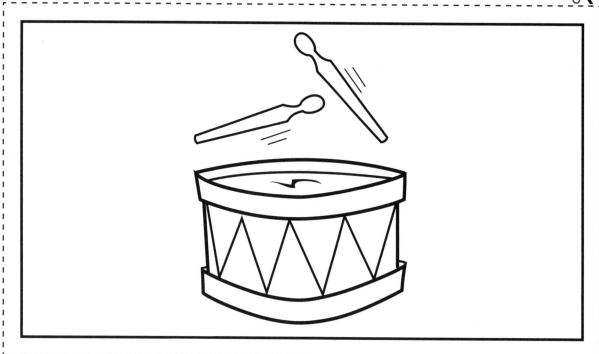

Letter Flashcard

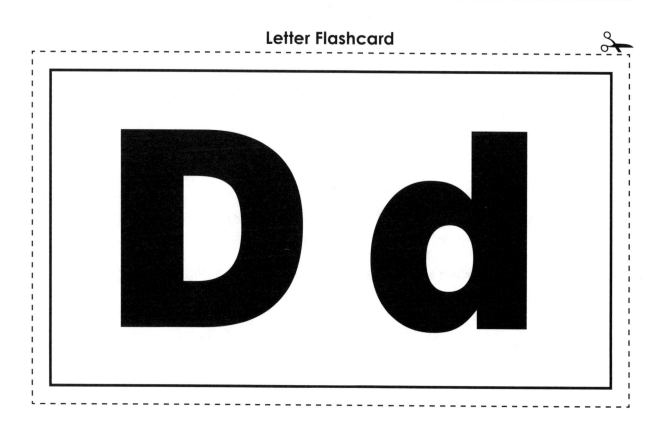

/d/ Flashcards

#BKCD-407 Webber® Hear It! Say It! Learn It!™ • ©2008 Super Duper® Publications • www.superduperinc.com • 1-800-277-8737

Drum Sound /d/
Auditory Bombardment Story

Directions: Read the story aloud to the student(s) or play it from the CD-ROM.

 Note: You have the option of having "No Text" (for auditory bombardment) or "Text" (for letter/word recognition and reading).

Donny Davidson's Drum

On his birthday, **D**onny **D**avidson's **d**ad gave him the present he had always **d**reamt about—a **d**rum! **D**onny was thrilled and **d**eclared the **d**ay to be his best birthday ever.

One **d**ay before breakfast, **D**onny marched around the house pounding his new **d**rum—**d**, **d**, **d**. Though **D**ad was **d**elighted **D**onny liked his **d**rum so much, it was time for **D**onny to sit **d**own to **d**ine. **D**ad told **D**onny, "Please stop pounding your **d**rum and sit **d**own to eat." But **D**onny **d**id not want to stop pounding on his **d**rum—**d**, **d**, **d**. So, he marched **d**ownstairs to the **d**en and then up to his bedroom. The loud **d**rum sound—**d**, **d**, **d**, woke **D**onny's baby brother, **D**illon. **D**onny's **d**ad calmed the baby **d**own and said, "**D**onny, maybe you should pound on your **d**rum outside in the yard. Then you can play as loud as you want." So **D**onny and his **d**rum headed outside.

Later that **d**ay, **D**onny's **d**ad was making **d**inner. Suddenly, he heard pounding much louder than **D**onny's **d**rum. He **d**arted over to the window and saw **D**onny marching **d**own the road with the neighborhood parade. The **d**, **d**, **d** sound of the **d**rums sounded wonderful. **D**onny's **d**ad was very proud of **D**onny. He waved and cheered as **D**onny marched and **d**rummed—**d**, **d**, **d**.

/d/ Auditory Bombardment

Drum Sound /d/ in Isolation

Directions: Give each student a copy of the **Drum Sound /d/ Worksheet 1**.

Say: *I'm going to say some sounds, one at a time. If you hear the **Drum Sound /d/**, put a check mark (✓) on the duck. If you hear a different sound, put an X on the duck. Ready? Number 1, /d/, Number 2, /d/, Number 3, /m/, etc.*

Use additional blank copies of **Worksheet 1** for the sound stimuli in Trial 2 and Trial 3 below. To record data for two or more students, see *Book 2, Appendix B*.

 For more practice, choose the **Drum Sound /d/** and complete the **Isolation** activity.

	Trial 1		Trial 2		Trial 3	
	Stimulus Sound	**Check if Correct** ✓	**Stimulus Sound**	**Check if Correct** ✓	**Stimulus Sound**	**Check if Correct** ✓
1.	/d/		/d/		/b/	
2.	/d/		/t/		/d/	
3.	/m/		/d/		/f/	
4.	/d/		/p/		/d/	
5.	/k/		/d/		/g/	
6.	/d/		/h/		/s/	
7.	/g/		/b/		/p/	
8.	/d/		/d/		/d/	
9.	/b/		/g/		/d/	
10.	/d/		/d/		/l/	
	Total:		**Total:**		**Total:**	

_____   _____
Student's Name   Date

Scoresheet 1
/d/ in Isolation

#BKCD-407 Webber® Hear It! Say It! Learn It!™ • ©2008 Super Duper® Publications • www.superduperinc.com • 1-800-277-8737

D d

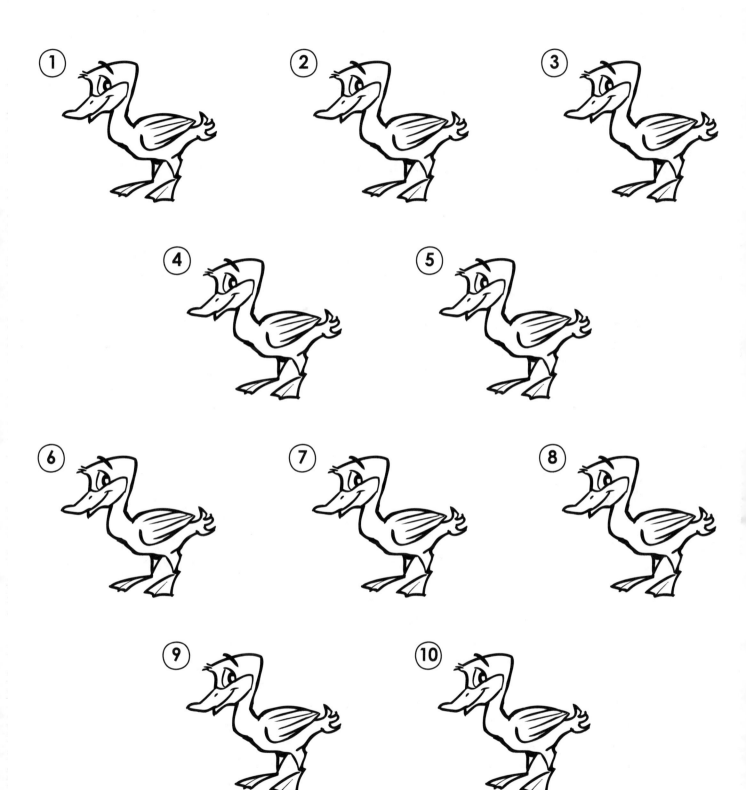

Drum Sound /d/ in Syllables

Directions: Give each student a copy of the **Drum Sound /d/ Worksheet 2**.

Say: *I'm going to say some silly words to you, one at a time. If you hear the* **Drum Sound /d/** *in the silly word, circle the dog. If you hear a different sound, put an X on the dog. Ready? Number 1, do-do, Number 2, po-po, Number 3, fo-fo, etc.*

Use additional blank copies of **Worksheet 2** for the sound stimuli in Trial 2 and Trial 3 below. To record data for two or more students, see *Book 2, Appendix B*.

 For more practice, choose the **Drum Sound /d/** and complete the **Syllables** activity.

	Trial 1		Trial 2		Trial 3	
	Stimulus Sound	**Check if Correct ✓**	**Stimulus Sound**	**Check if Correct ✓**	**Stimulus Sound**	**Check if Correct ✓**
1.	do-do		do-do		dee-dee	
2.	po-po		da-da		ma-ma	
3.	fo-fo		mo-mo		bo-bo	
4.	do-do		ga-ga		da-da	
5.	go-go		do-do		la-la	
6.	lo-lo		da-da		do-do	
7.	bo-bo		ba-ba		nee-nee	
8.	do-do		lo-lo		ba-ba	
9.	do-do		do-do		go-go	
10.	mo-mo		go-go		loo-loo	
	Total:		**Total:**		**Total:**	

_____   _____
Student's Name   Date

Scoresheet 2 /d/ in Syllables

#BKCD-407 Webber® Hear It! Say It! Learn It!™ • ©2008 Super Duper® Publications • www.superduperinc.com • 1-800-277-8737

D d

  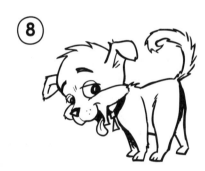

_____ _____

Name   Date

Worksheet 2
/d/ in Syllables

Drum Sound /d/ in Pictures

Directions: Give each student a copy of the **Drum Sound /d/ Worksheet 3**.

Say: *I'm going to say some words to you. Listen to me say two words each time. If you hear the **Drum Sound /d/** at the beginning of the word, circle the picture that begins with the **Drum Sound /d/**. Ready? Number 1, dog - ball, Number 2, bus - dust, Number 3, desk - can, etc.*

To record data for two or more students, see *Book 2, Appendix B*.

 For more practice, choose the **Drum Sound /d/** and complete the **Pictures** activity.

	Word Pair		Check if Correct ✓
1.	**d**og	ball	
2.	bus	**d**ust	
3.	**d**esk	can	
4.	**d**ig	book	
5.	nail	**d**ot	
6.	**d**ive	mouse	
7.	sun	**d**ime	
8.	**d**oor	pot	
9.	**d**uck	ham	
10.	cake	**d**oll	
		Total:	

_____   _____
Student's Name   Date

#BKCD-407 Webber® Hear It! Say It! Learn It!™ • ©2008 Super Duper® Publications • www.superduperinc.com • 1-800-277-8737

D d

Learning to Write the Letter Dd

Directions: Introduce the letter **Dd**. Have the student(s) cut out the Letter Flashcard from page 126 and glue or tape the backs of the two flashcards (Picture Symbol and Letter) together. Now, student(s) can refer to **both** sides of the flashcard for reinforcement during the remainder of the chapter.

Say: *This is the letter **Dd**. This (point) is the uppercase **D**. This is the lowercase **d**. The letter **Dd** makes the **Drum Sound /d/**. What is the Drum Sound?*

Have the student(s) practice forming uppercase **D** and lowercase **d** using the index finger of his/her dominant hand to trace the letters on the flashcards. Demonstrate the action first.

Say: *To make an uppercase **D**, put your finger at the top of the letter. Make a straight line down, like a stick. Pick up your finger and put it back at the top. Make a big bubble, from the top to the bottom of the stick.*

*To make a lowercase **d**, put your finger at the top of the letter. Make a line straight line down, like a stick. Make a small bubble attached to the bottom of the stick.*

Note: You may need to modify letter formation and/or verbal cues to best fit with your school's curriculum. For a quick guide to handwriting cues, refer to *Book 2, Appendix C*.

Give each student a copy of the **Drum Sound /d/ Worksheet 4**. Student(s) will practice writing uppercase **D** and lowercase **d** with a pencil. First, have the student(s) trace within the outlines. Then, trace along the dotted lines. Finally, have the student(s) practice writing the letter without a guide.

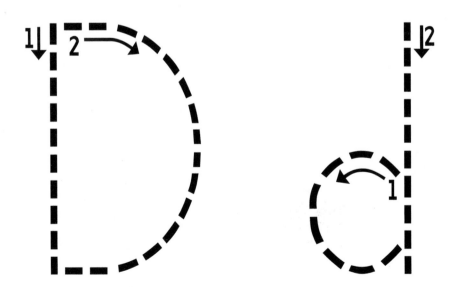

Learning to Write the Letter Dd

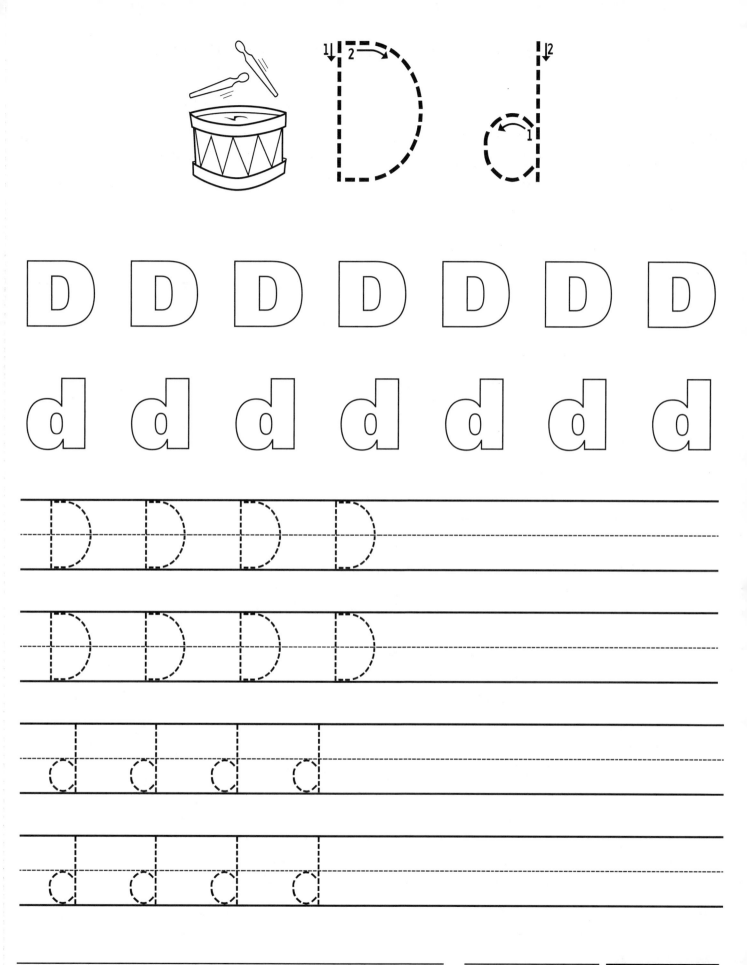

Name _____   Date _____

Worksheet 4
Writing Dd

#BKCD-407 Webber® Hear It! Say It! Learn It!™ • ©2008 Super Duper® Publications • www.superduperinc.com • 1-800-277-8737

Drum Sound /d/ and Letter Dd in Pictures with Initial Letter

Directions: Give each student a copy of the **Drum Sound /d/ Worksheet 5**.

Say: *I'm going to say some words. Listen to me say two words each time. If you hear the* **Drum Sound /d/** *at the beginning of the word <u>and</u> see the letter* **Dd***, circle the picture and letter that begins with the* **Drum Sound /d/***. Ready? Number 1, deer - tie, Number 2, bell - door, Number 3, moose - dog, etc.*

To record data for two or more students, see *Book 2, Appendix B.*

 For more practice, choose the **Drum Sound /d/** and complete the **Pictures & Letters** activity.

	Word Pair		Check if Correct ✓
1.	**d**eer	tie	
2.	Bell	**D**oor	
3.	moose	**d**og	
4.	**d**ate	cap	
5.	Feet	**D**uck	
6.	**D**ish	Tire	
7.	bug	**d**ive	
8.	Mug	**D**ot	
9.	**d**oll	van	
10.	Girl	**D**esk	
		Total:	

_____   _____

Student's Name   Date

Scoresheet 5 /d/ in Pictures

136   #BKCD-407 Webber® Hear It! Say It! Learn It!™ • ©2008 Super Duper® Publications • www.superduperinc.com • 1-800-277-8737

D d

1.		d			t
2.		B			D
3.		m			d
4.		d			c
5.		F			D
6.		D			T
7.		b			d
8.		M			D
9.		d			V
10.		G			D

_____   _____
Name   Date

#BKCD-407 Webber® Hear It! Say It! Learn It!™ • ©2008 Super Duper® Publications • www.superduperinc.com • 1-800-277-8737

Practice Writing the Letter Dd

Directions: Give each student a copy of the **Drum Sound /d/ Worksheet 6**.

Say: *I'm going to say some sounds, one at a time. If you hear the **Drum Sound /d/**, write an uppercase **D** in the donut. If you hear a different sound, put an X in the donut. Ready? Donut Number 1, /d/, Number 2, /f/, Number 3, /d/, etc.*

Practice writing a lowercase **d** using Trial 2 stimuli on an additional copy of **Worksheet 6**. To record data for two or more students, see *Book 2, Appendix B*.

	Trial 1			Trial 2		
	Stimulus Sound	Correctly Identified /d/ Sound	Correctly Wrote Uppercase D	Stimulus Sound	Correctly Identified /d/ Sound	Correctly Wrote Lowercase d
1.	/d/			/d/		
2.	/f/			/g/		
3.	/d/			/w/		
4.	/m/			/d/		
5.	/d/			/d/		
6.	/g/			/v/		
7.	/p/			/d/		
8.	/d/			/n/		
9.	/d/			/d/		
10.	/s/			/t/		
	Total:			Total:		

_____   _____

Student's Name   Date

**Scoresheet 6
Writing Dd**

#BKCD-407 Webber® Hear It! Say It! Learn It!™ • ©2008 Super Duper® Publications • www.superduperinc.com • 1-800-277-8737

Trial _____

D d

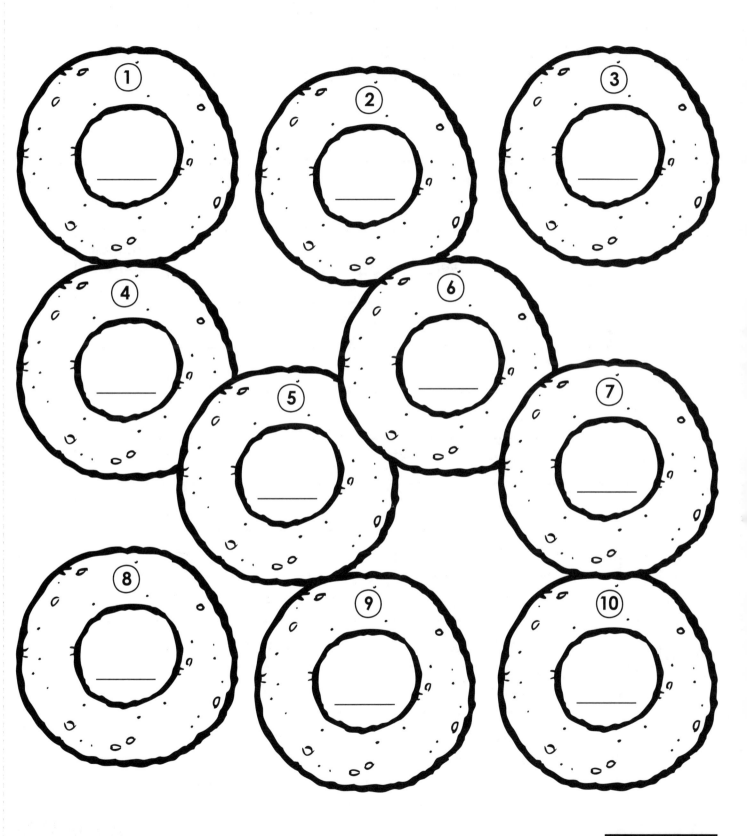

#BKCD-407 Webber® Hear It! Say It! Learn It!™ • ©2008 Super Duper® Publications • www.superduperinc.com • 1-800-277-8737

Drum Sound /d/ and Letter Dd in Pictures and Words

Directions: Give each student a copy of the **Drum Sound /d/ Worksheet 7**.

Say: *On this paper, we see pictures with words beside them. Look at the pictures and words on the first row. Say the word that names each picture. If the word starts with the* **Drum Sound /d/** <u>and</u> *you see the letter* **Dd**, *put a circle on that picture. Ready? Number 1, duck - luck, Number 2, dot - pot, Number 3, log - dog, etc.*

To record data for two or more students, see *Book 2, Appendix B.*

 For more practice, choose the **Drum Sound /d/** and complete the **Pictures & Words** activity.

	Word Pair		Check if Correct ✓
1.	**D**uck	Luck	
2.	**D**ot	Pot	
3.	log	**d**og	
4.	**d**oor	floor	
5.	**d**oe	toe	
6.	gate	**d**ate	
7.	Time	**D**ime	
8.	pig	**d**ig	
9.	**D**art	Cart	
10.	Hive	**D**ive	
		Total:	

_____   _____
Student's Name   Date

#BKCD-407 Webber® Hear It! Say It! Learn It!™ • ©2008 Super Duper® Publications • www.superduperinc.com • 1-800-277-8737

D d

1.		**D**uck			Luck
2.		**D**ot			Pot
3.		log			**d**og
4.		**d**oor			floor
5.		**d**oe			toe
6.		gate			**d**ate
7.		Time			**D**ime
8.		pig			**d**ig
9.		**D**art			Cart
10.		Hive			**D**ive

#BKCD-407 Webber® Hear It! Say It! Learn It!™ • ©2008 Super Duper® Publications • www.superduperinc.com • 1-800-277-8737

Drum Sound /d/ and the Letter Dd in Words

Directions: Give each student a copy of the **Drum Sound /d/ Worksheet 8**.

Say: *On this paper, we see a list of words. Some of them begin with the letter **Dd** which makes the **Drum Sound /d/**. I'm going to say two words each time. Point to each word as I say it. Circle the word that begins with the letter **Dd** and the **Drum Sound /d/**. Ready? Number 1, date - late, Number 2, dip - sip, Number 3, camp - damp, etc.*

To record data for two or more students, see *Book 2, Appendix B*.

 For more practice, choose the **Drum Sound /d/** and complete the **Words** activity.

	Word Pair		Check if Correct ✓
1.	**d**ate	late	
2.	**d**ip	sip	
3.	Camp	**D**amp	
4.	**d**are	fare	
5.	Line	**D**ine	
6.	maze	**d**aze	
7.	**D**ay	Way	
8.	pie	**d**ie	
9.	lot	**d**ot	
10.	**D**uck	Buck	
		Total:	

_____   _____

Student's Name   Date

 # D d

1.	date	late
2.	dip	sip
3.	Camp	Damp
4.	dare	fare
5.	Line	Dine
6.	maze	daze
7.	Day	Way
8.	pie	die
9.	lot	dot
10.	Duck	Buck

Name _____ Date _____

#BKCD-407 Webber® Hear It! Say It! Learn It!™ • ©2008 Super Duper® Publications • www.superduperinc.com • 1-800-277-8737

Extension Activity for the Drum Sound /d/

Have the students engage in a dancing activity modeled after the game "Simon Says." Have the class dance at different rates and with a variety of movements. For example, say to the students, "Simon says—dance fast." Then after a few moments, change the motion by saying, "Simon says—dance slowly." Randomly give directions without saying, "Simon says." For example, you may say, "Dance with your hands above your head." If any students dance with their hands above their heads, they need to sit down, because you did not say, "Simon says."

Say: Follow the directions if you hear me say, "Simon says." If you don't hear me say, "Simon says," don't follow the directions.

After completing the activity, gather the class around a story chart or chalkboard. Ask the students to tell you about the activity. Write their comments on the chart/board. Then, read the sentences together. You should not expect the students to be able to read the story, but they will begin to connect fluent speech with written text and recognize words beginning with the target sound.

Lead the students through a retelling of the activity in the following manner:

1. If possible, use a tape recorder to record the students' sentences about the activity.

2. Replay the taped sentences and write them on the board.

3. After writing each sentence, read each sentence once.

4. Have the class "read" the sentences a second time along with you.

5. As the students read the sentences aloud, move a pointer (or your finger) in a continuous, fluid motion across the words.

6. Encourage the students to come up one by one and point to any words that begin with the target sound and letter (**Drum Sound /d/**).

See example sentences for this activity below.

"We **danced** fast."

"We **danced** slowly."

"We **danced** when Simon said to **dance**."

"**Danny** had to sit **down**."

Create your own activity and story using the **Drum Sound /d/**!

**Extension Activity
Drum Sound /d/**

Rooster Sound /k/
Introducing the Rooster Sound /k/

Introduce the **Rooster Sound /k/** by reading the script below to the student(s). Demonstrate and discuss the formation of the Rooster Sound (see *Resource Book 2*, Appendix A for a description of the **Rooster Sound /k/**).

Say: *Today we are going to learn about the* **Rooster Sound /k/**. *Watch me say the* **Rooster Sound**: */k/ (pause) /k/ (pause) /k/. Now it's your turn to make the* **Rooster Sound /k/**.

Have the students practice the **Rooster Sound /k/** aloud. Then, ask the questions in the table below.

Lips	*What are your lips doing when you say the* **Rooster Sound /k/**?
Tongue	*Do you use your tongue to say the* **Rooster Sound /k/**?
Breath	*Is there a burst of air or a long flow of air when you say the* **Rooster Sound /k/**?
Voice	*Feel your neck when you say the* **Rooster Sound /k/**. *Can you feel any vibration? That is because the* **Rooster Sound /k/** *does not have voice.*

Have the student(s) cut out the Picture Symbol Flashcard on page 146. Student(s) can refer to this picture symbol for reinforcement during the Auditory Bombardment Story and throughout the first part of the chapter (Worksheets 1–3).

Note: You will be prompted to create the Letter Flashcard with Worksheet 4.

Kk/Cc

Picture Symbol Flashcard

Letter Flashcard

Kk/Cc

#BKCD-407 Webber® Hear It! Say It! Learn It!™ • ©2008 Super Duper® Publications • www.superduperinc.com • 1-800-277-8737

Rooster Sound /k/
Auditory Bombardment Story

Directions: Read the story aloud to the student(s) or play it from the CD-ROM.

 Note: You have the option of having "No Text" (for auditory bombardment) or "Text" (for letter/word recognition and reading).

Kelsey Cassidy and Calvin

Once there was a **c**ute little **k**id named **K**elsey **C**assidy. One **c**alm morning, **K**elsey woke up to the sound of her **c**razy rooster, **C**alvin, **c**rooning, "*k, k, k*." **K**elsey **c**ould not **c**omprehend why **C**alvin was making a *k, k, k* sound because he usually woke everyone up with a "**c**ock-a-doodle-doo." **K**elsey was very **c**oncerned about **C**alvin.

Kelsey ran to her parents' room and said, "Mommy and Daddy, there is something wrong with **C**alvin. He is not saying '**c**ock-a-doodle-doo' like he normally does. He is **c**rooning '*k, k, k*.'" **K**elsey's parents, **K**ay and **K**yle **C**assidy, just chuckled. They **c**onsoled her, "**K**elsey, do not worry about **C**alvin. He is fine," they said. "**C**alvin is just tired of **c**rowing '**c**ock-a-doodle-doo' every morning. He needed a change."

Now, when **K**elsey **C**assidy, the **c**ute little **k**id, wakes up each morning, she occasionally hears **C**alvin **c**row, "**c**ock-a-doodle-doo." Sometimes she hears **C**alvin **c**roon, "*k, k, k*." But no matter what sound her **c**razy rooster **C**alvin makes, **K**elsey, **K**ay, and **K**yle **C**assidy all know it is time to rise and shine and begin their day.

Rooster Sound /k/ in Isolation

Directions: Give each student a copy of the **Rooster Sound /k/ Worksheet 1**.

Say: *I'm going to say some sounds, one at a time. If you hear the **Rooster Sound /k/**, put a check mark (✓) on the kite. If you hear a different sound, put an X on the kite. Ready? Number 1, /k/, Number 2, /k/, Number 3, /m/, etc.*

Use additional blank copies of **Worksheet 1** for the sound stimuli in Trial 2 and Trial 3 below. To record data for two or more students, see *Book 2, Appendix B*.

 For more practice, choose the **Rooster Sound /k/** and complete the **Isolation** activity.

	Trial 1		**Trial 2**		**Trial 3**	
	Stimulus Sound	**Check if Correct** ✓	**Stimulus Sound**	**Check if Correct** ✓	**Stimulus Sound**	**Check if Correct** ✓
1.	/k/		/k/		/k/	
2.	/k/		/n/		/f/	
3.	/m/		/k/		/k/	
4.	/s/		/t/		/p/	
5.	/k/		/k/		/m/	
6.	/k/		/k/		/k/	
7.	/d/		/d/		/k/	
8.	/k/		/k/		/t/	
9.	/p/		/f/		/k/	
10.	/k/		/k/		/k/	
	Total:		**Total:**		**Total:**	

_____   _____

Student's Name   Date

Scoresheet 1 /k/ in Isolation

#BKCD-407 Webber® Hear It! Say It! Learn It!™ • ©2008 Super Duper® Publications • www.superduperinc.com • 1-800-277-8737

Kk/Cc

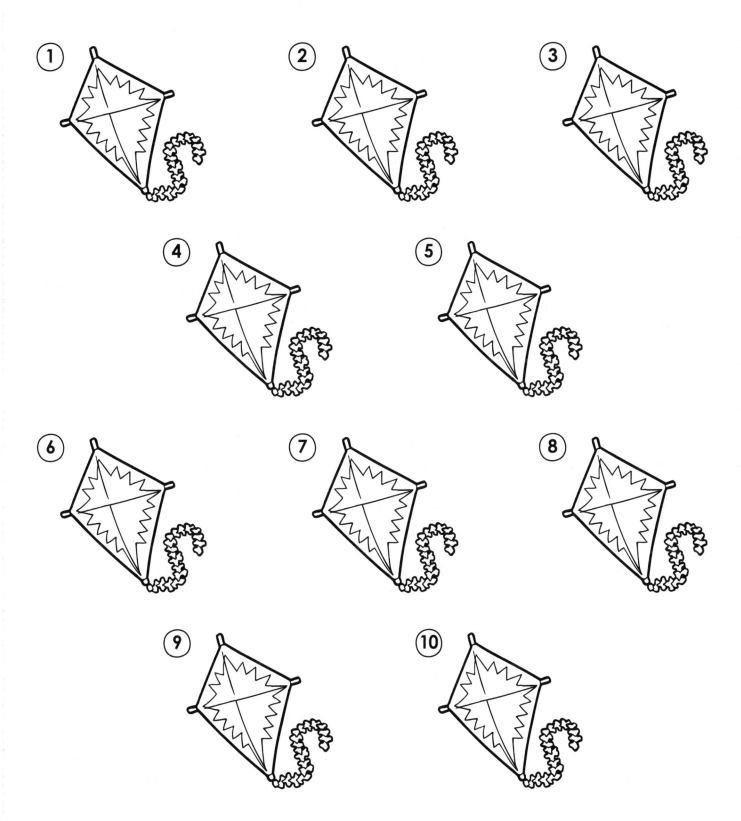

Rooster Sound /k/ in Syllables

Directions: Give each student a copy of the **Rooster Sound /k/ Worksheet 2**.

Say: *I'm going to say some silly words to you, one at a time. If you hear the **Rooster Sound /k/** in the silly word, circle the cat. If you hear a different sound, put an X on the cat. Ready? Number 1, ko-ko, Number 2, so-so, Number 3, ko-ko, etc.*

Use additional blank copies of **Worksheet 2** for the sound stimuli in Trial 2 and Trial 3 below. To record data for two or more students, see *Book 2, Appendix B*.

 For more practice, choose the **Rooster Sound /k/** and complete the **Syllables** activity.

	Trial 1		Trial 2		Trial 3	
	Stimulus Sound	**Check if Correct** ✓	**Stimulus Sound**	**Check if Correct** ✓	**Stimulus Sound**	**Check if Correct** ✓
1.	ko-ko		ko-ko		kee-kee	
2.	so-so		see-see		sa-sa	
3.	ko-ko		to-to		fo-fo	
4.	ko-ko		kee-kee		koo-koo	
5.	mo-mo		po-po		ko-ko	
6.	lo-lo		kee-kee		tay-tay	
7.	ko-ko		ko-ko		loo-loo	
8.	po-po		lee-lee		kay-kay	
9.	ko-ko		go-go		go-go	
10.	ko-ko		kee-kee		ko-ko	
	Total:		**Total:**		**Total:**	

_____   _____   **Scoresheet 2**
Student's Name   Date   **/k/ in Syllables**

#BKCD-407 Webber® Hear It! Say It! Learn It!™ • ©2008 Super Duper® Publications • www.superduperinc.com • 1-800-277-8737

Kk/Cc

①  ②  ③

④  ⑤

⑥  ⑦  ⑧

⑨  ⑩

Name _____ Date _____

Worksheet 2
/k/ in Syllables

Rooster Sound /k/ in Pictures

Directions: Give each student a copy of the **Rooster Sound /k/ Worksheet 3**.

Say: *I'm going to say some words to you. Listen to me say two words each time. If you hear the **Rooster Sound /k/** at the beginning of the word, circle the picture that begins with the **Rooster Sound /k/**. Ready? Number 1, kite - sun, Number 2, bat - cup, Number 3, car - rope, etc.*

To record data for two or more students, see *Book 2, Appendix B*.

 For more practice, choose the **Rooster Sound /k/** and complete the **Pictures** activity.

	Word Pair		Check if Correct ✓
1.	**k**ite	sun	
2.	bat	**c**up	
3.	**c**ar	rope	
4.	**k**ey	moon	
5.	doll	**c**oat	
6.	feet	**c**orn	
7.	horse	**k**id	
8.	**c**ap	goose	
9.	bug	**c**an	
10.	**c**at	nest	
		Total:	

_____   _____
Student's Name   Date

#BKCD-407 Webber® Hear It! Say It! Learn It!™ • ©2008 Super Duper® Publications • www.superduperinc.com • 1-800-277-8737

Scoresheet 3 /k/ in Pictures

Kk/Cc

1.			6.			
2.			7.			
3.			8.			
4.			9.			
5.			10.			

_____
Name

_____
Date

Learning to Write the Letter Kk

Directions: Introduce the letter **Kk**. Have the student(s) cut out the Letter Flashcard from page 146 and glue or tape the backs of the two flashcards (Picture Symbol and Letter) together. Now, student(s) can refer to **both** sides of the flashcard for reinforcement during the remainder of the chapter.

Say: *This is the letter **Kk**. This (point) is the uppercase **K**. This is the lowercase **k**. The letter **Kk** makes the **Rooster Sound /k/**. What is the Rooster Sound?*

Have the student(s) practice forming uppercase **K** and lowercase **k** using the index finger of his/her dominant hand to trace the letters on the flashcards. Demonstrate the action first.

Say: *To make an uppercase **K**, put your finger at the top of the letter. Make a straight line down, like a stick. Make a slanted line from the top to the middle of the stick. Make another slanted line to the bottom.*

*To make a lowercase **k**, put your finger at the top of the letter. Make a line straight line down, like a stick. Make a slanted line toward the bottom of the stick. Make another slanted line to the bottom.*

Note: You may need to modify letter formation and/or verbal cues to best fit with your school's curriculum. For a quick guide to handwriting cues, refer to *Book 2, Appendix C*.

Give each student a copy of the **Rooster Sound /k/ Worksheet 4.1**. Student(s) will practice writing uppercase **K** and lowercase **k** with a pencil. First, have the student(s) trace within the outlines. Then, trace along the dotted lines. Finally, have the student(s) practice writing the letter without a guide.

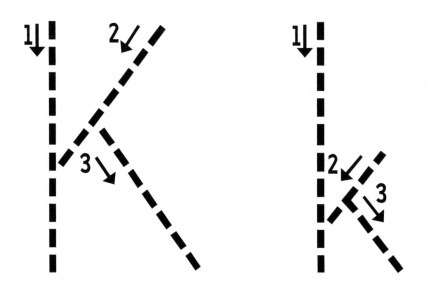

**Learning to Write
the Letter Kk**

#BKCD-407 Webber® Hear It! Say It! Learn It!™ • ©2008 Super Duper® Publications • www.superduperinc.com • 1-800-277-8737

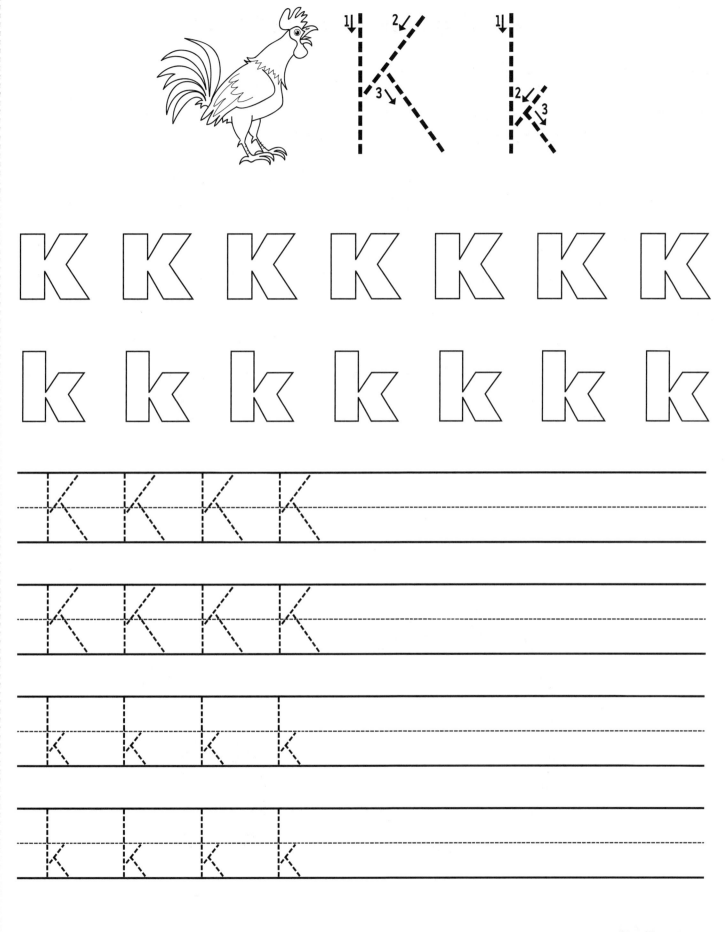

#BKCD-407 Webber® Hear It! Say It! Learn It!™ • ©2008 Super Duper® Publications • www.superduperinc.com • 1-800-277-8737

Learning to Write the Letter Cc

Directions: Introduce the letter **Cc**. Have the student(s) refer to the flashcards from page 146.

Say: *This is the letter **Cc**. This (point) is the uppercase **C**. This is the lowercase **c**. The letter **Cc** makes the **Rooster Sound /k/**. What is the Rooster Sound?*

Have the student(s) practice forming uppercase **C** and lowercase **c** using the index finger of his/her dominant hand to trace the letters on the flashcards. Demonstrate the action first.

Say: *To make an uppercase **C**, put your finger at the top of the letter. Make part of a bubble.*

*To make a lowercase **c**, put your finger at the top of the letter. Make part of a small bubble.*

Note: You may need to modify letter formation and/or verbal cues to best fit with your school's curriculum. For a quick guide to handwriting cues, refer to *Book 2, Appendix C*.

Give each student a copy of the **Rooster Sound /k/ Worksheet 4.2**. Student(s) will practice writing uppercase **C** and lowercase **c** with a pencil. First, have the student(s) trace within the outlines. Then, trace along the dotted lines. Finally, have the student(s) practice writing the letter without a guide.

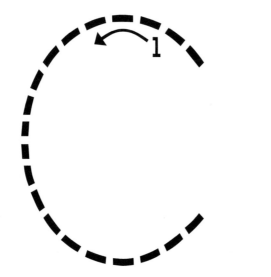

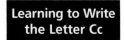

Name _____ Date _____

Worksheet 4.2
Writing Cc

#BKCD-407 Webber® Hear It! Say It! Learn It!™ • ©2008 Super Duper® Publications • www.superduperinc.com • 1-800-277-8737

Rooster Sound /k/ and Letters Kk and Cc in Pictures with Initial Letter

Directions: Give each student a copy of the **Rooster Sound /k/ Worksheet 5.**

Say: *I'm going to say some words. Listen to me say two words each time. If you hear the Rooster Sound /k/ at the beginning of the word and see the letter Kk or the letter Cc, circle the picture and letter that begins with the Rooster Sound /k/. Ready? Number 1, key - hat, Number 2, nail - call, Number 3, cat - rock, etc.*

To record data for two or more students, see *Book 2, Appendix B.*

 For more practice, choose the **Rooster Sound /k/** and complete the **Pictures & Letters** activity.

	Word Pair		Check if Correct ✓
1.	**k**ey	hat	
2.	nail	**c**all	
3.	**C**at	Rock	
4.	Pen	**K**ing	
5.	fish	**c**up	
6.	**c**age	nest	
7.	bug	**k**ite	
8.	**C**orn	Goose	
9.	Rope	**K**iss	
10.	**c**an	wash	
		Total:	

_____   _____
Student's Name   Date

#BKCD-407 Webber® Hear It! Say It! Learn It!™ • ©2008 Super Duper® Publications • www.superduperinc.com • 1-800-277-8737

Kk/Cc

1.		k		h
2.		n		c
3.		C		R
4.		P		K
5.		f		c
6.		c		n
7.		b		k
8.		C		G
9.		R		K
10.		c		w

Name _____   Date _____

#BKCD-407 Webber® Hear It! Say It! Learn It!™ • ©2008 Super Duper® Publications • www.superduperinc.com • 1-800-277-8737

Practice Writing the Letter Kk

Directions: Give each student a copy of the **Rooster Sound /k/ Worksheet 6**.

Say: *I'm going to say some sounds, one at a time. If you hear the **Rooster Sound /k/**, write an uppercase **K** on the key. If you hear a different sound, put an X on the key. Ready? Key Number 1, /k/, Number 2, /k/, Number 3, /m/, etc.*

Practice writing a lowercase **k** using Trial 2 stimuli on an additional copy of **Worksheet 6.1**. To record data for two or more students, see *Book 2, Appendix B*.

	Trial 1			Trial 2		
	Stimulus Sound	**Correctly Identified /k/ Sound**	**Correctly Wrote Uppercase K**	**Stimulus Sound**	**Correctly Identified /k/ Sound**	**Correctly Wrote Lowercase k**
1.	/k/			/k/		
2.	/k/			/l/		
3.	/m/			/k/		
4.	/k/			/h/		
5.	/f/			/k/		
6.	/s/			/g/		
7.	/k/			/k/		
8.	/t/			/p/		
9.	/h/			/k/		
10.	/k/			/d/		
	Total:			**Total:**		

_____   _____

Student's Name   Date

#BKCD-407 Webber® Hear It! Say It! Learn It!™ • ©2008 Super Duper® Publications • www.superduperinc.com • 1-800-277-8737

K k

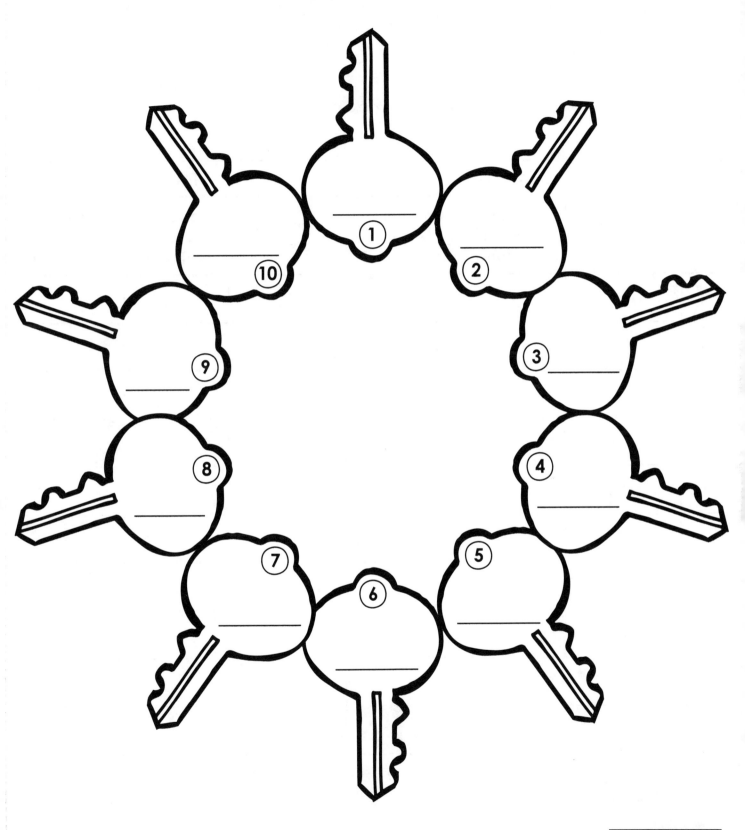

#BKCD-407 Webber® Hear It! Say It! Learn It!™ • ©2008 Super Duper® Publications • www.superduperinc.com • 1-800-277-8737

Practice Writing the Letter Cc

Directions: Give each student a copy of the **Rooster Sound /k/ Worksheet 6**.

Say: *I'm going to say some sounds, one at a time. If you hear the **Rooster Sound /k/**, write an uppercase **C** on the cupcake. If you hear a different sound, put an X on the cupcake. Ready? Cupcake Number 1, /k/, Number 2, /f/, Number 3, /k/, etc.*

Practice writing a lowercase **c** using Trial 2 stimuli on an additional copy of **Worksheet 6.2**. To record data for two or more students, see *Book 2, Appendix B*.

	Trial 1			Trial 2		
	Stimulus Sound	**Correctly Identified /k/ Sound**	**Correctly Wrote Uppercase C**	**Stimulus Sound**	**Correctly Identified /k/ Sound**	**Correctly Wrote Lowercase c**
1.	/k/			/k/		
2.	/f/		▒	/l/		▒
3.	/k/			/k/		
4.	/k/		▒	/h/		▒
5.	/g/			/k/		
6.	/l/		▒	/g/		▒
7.	/k/		▒	/k/		
8.	/k/			/p/		▒
9.	/p/			/k/		
10.	/s/		▒	/d/		▒
	Total:			**Total:**		

_____   _____

Student's Name   Date

#BKCD-407 Webber® Hear It! Say It! Learn It!™ • ©2008 Super Duper® Publications • www.superduperinc.com • 1-800-277-8737

C c

Trial _____

Name _____

Date _____

Worksheet 6.2
Writing Cc

Rooster Sound /k/ and Letters Kk and Cc in Pictures and Words

Directions: Give each student a copy of the **Rooster Sound /k/ Worksheet 7**.

Say: *On this paper, we see pictures with words beside them. Look at the pictures and words on the first row. Say the word that names each picture. If the word starts with the* **Rooster Sound /k/** <u>and</u> *you see the letter* **Kk** *or the letter* **Cc**, *put a circle on that picture. Ready? Number 1, kite - bite, Number 2, miss - kiss, Number 3, hat - cat, etc.*

To record data for two or more students, see *Book 2, Appendix B.*

 For more practice, choose the **Rooster Sound /k/** and complete the **Pictures & Words** activity.

	Word Pair		Check if Correct ✓
1.	**K**ite	Bite	
2.	miss	**k**iss	
3.	Hat	**C**at	
4.	fan	**c**an	
5.	**K**id	Lid	
6.	**C**amp	Lamp	
7.	horn	**c**orn	
8.	map	**c**ap	
9.	**c**ave	wave	
10.	**C**all	Ball	
		Total:	

_____   _____
Student's Name   Date

#BKCD-407 Webber® Hear It! Say It! Learn It!™ • ©2008 Super Duper® Publications • www.superduperinc.com • 1-800-277-8737

 # Kk/Cc

1.		**K**ite		Bite
2.		miss		**k**iss
3.		Hat		**C**at
4.		fan		**c**an
5.		**K**id		Lid
6.		**C**amp		Lamp
7.		horn		**c**orn
8.		map		**c**ap
9.		**c**ave		wave
10.		**C**all		Ball

Name _____   Date _____

Worksheet 7
/k/ in Pictures
and Words

Rooster Sound /k/ and the Letters Kk and Cc in Words

Directions: Give each student a copy of the **Rooster Sound /k/ Worksheet 8**.

Say: *On this paper, we see a list of words. Some of them begin with the letter **Kk** or the letter **Cc** which make the **Rooster Sound /k/**. I'm going to say two words each time. Point to each word as I say it. Circle the word that begins with the letter **Kk** or the letter **Cc** and the **Rooster Sound /k/**. Ready? Number 1, did - kid, Number 2, coin - join, Number 3, kit - sit, etc.*

To record data for two or more students, see *Book 2, Appendix B*.

For more practice, choose the **Rooster Sound /k/** and complete the **Words** activity.

	Word Pair		Check if Correct ✓
1.	did	**k**id	
2.	**C**oin	Join	
3.	**K**it	Sit	
4.	man	**c**an	
5.	**c**old	mold	
6.	**k**ind	mind	
7.	hop	**c**op	
8.	**C**ut	Nut	
9.	**K**iss	Miss	
10.	mane	**c**ane	
		Total:	

_____   _____
Student's Name   Date

#BKCD-407 Webber® Hear It! Say It! Learn It!™ • ©2008 Super Duper® Publications • www.superduperinc.com • 1-800-277-8737

Kk/Cc

1.	did	kid
2.	Coin	Join
3.	Kit	Sit
4.	man	can
5.	cold	mold
6.	kind	mind
7.	hop	cop
8.	Cut	Nut
9.	Kiss	Miss
10.	mane	cane

_____   _____
Name   Date

#BKCD-407 Webber® Hear It! Say It! Learn It!™ • ©2008 Super Duper® Publications • www.superduperinc.com • 1-800-277-8737

Extension Activity for the Rooster Sound /k/

Use construction paper, pipe cleaners, string, and glue to make small paper kites. Let the students be creative with the shape and colors of their kites—it is not necessary for the kites to fly. Below is an example of how to construct a paper kite.

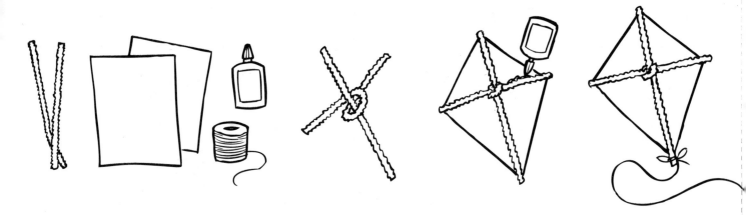

After completing the activity, gather the class around a story chart or chalkboard. Ask the students to tell you about the activity. Write their comments on the chart/board. Then, read the sentences together. You should not expect the students to be able to read the story, but they will begin to connect fluent speech with written text and recognize words beginning with the target sound.

Lead the students through a retelling of the activity in the following manner:

1. If possible, use a tape recorder to record the students' sentences about the activity.

2. Replay the taped sentences and write them on the board.

3. After writing each sentence, read each sentence once.

4. Have the class "read" the sentences a second time along with you.

5. As the students read the sentences aloud, move a pointer (or your finger) in a continuous, fluid motion across the words.

6. Encourage the students to come up one by one and point to any words that begin with the target sound and letter (**Rooster Sound /k/**).

See example sentences for this activity below.

"We **crafted** paper **kites**."   "We tied a **cord** to the **kite**."

"**Cara's kite** is **colorful**."   "Lindsay's **kite** has the most **colors**."

Create your own activity and story using the **Rooster Sound /k/!**

**Extension Activity
Rooster Sound /k/**

#BKCD-407 Webber® Hear It! Say It! Learn It!™ • ©2008 Super Duper® Publications • www.superduperinc.com • 1-800-277-8737